IN THE BEGINNING
Vol. 1

Ancient History, Religion, Starseed Origins, and Ascension

SHAKINAH RAY

In the Beginning Vol. 1

Copyright © 2024 by Shakinah Ray

No part of this book may be reproduced in any form or by any means, electronic or mechanical, including photocopying, recording, or by any information storage and retrieval system, without permission in writing from the publisher.

ISBN: 979-8-218-46705-0 Paperback

Dedicated to

The Ancestors and
the incoming children
born with full consciousness
making it possible for all Humans to
return to the Tao
and the New Dream.

May we continue to lift ourselves and each other up
to heal those before us and after us.

Books I and II Synopsis

Volume 1. Volume I takes readers through a journey of Egyptian history, exploring the Atenist movement, delving into Egyptian religion, examining the Keepers of the Blue Flame during the first exodus, offering a new perspective on Christ consciousness and Jesheua-12/Tutankhamen, discussing Christianity and the Druids/Gnostics, interpreting Jeshua-9 Elohim Avatar, and analyzing ascension.

Volume 2. In the second volume, we delve into the Sixth Dimensional Royal House, which covers Egyptian history and the Annanuki (Greek & Roman gods). The focus is on myths of various gods and goddesses throughout history, with a particular emphasis on Jeshua-9/Jesus as a man (Jesus Christ), the Essenes, Druids/Gnostics, and understanding reincarnation. Book II also delves into Magicians and healers by examining the Knights Templar, Freemasons, Essenes, Cathars, and Mandeans. The text discusses how the first seeded Humans transitioned from a magnetic to electrical energy signature.

Autobiography of a Starseed. The 3rd book in this series, *Autobiography of a Starseed*, tells the story of Shakinah's ascension path, multiple lives, and soul mission. She shares her recollections and the reasons she incarnated to this period of Earth.

About the Author: Shakinah is an author, spiritual channel, and international workshop presenter. As a globally recognized speaker and intuitive, she has impacted lives around the world through her Advanced Soul Purpose Workshops (ASPWs). In her books, *In the Beginning*, Volumes 1 and 2, Shakinah guides readers on a profound historical journey—tracing back to the dawn of time, exploring our Starseed origins, and unveiling humanity's connection with our star brothers and sisters. Through her writings and workshops, she offers insight into the current ascension process, helping others navigate this transformative era.

DISCLAIMER

The experiences and viewpoints expressed in this book are the author's subjective ones; the information is not accurate for everyone.

REVIEWS

We have passed through the end times of the 3D Matrix as predicted by the Mayan Calendar (around 2012) and we are now in the transition time of awakening where starseeds are waking up and leading the way to a New Age of Wisdom and Light. In this Age we are waking up to our true multidimensional heritage and to the importance of creating wise relations with all the kingdoms of the Earth. This book is an aid to the ascension process. It takes us on a historical journey that stretches back to the very beginning of time, to our starseed origins and our planet's relationship with Her star brothers and sisters. This is essentially a channeled book revealing many mysteries including our ancient connection to the Annanuki races, the Sirians, Lyrans, and Arcturians.

Steve Ahnael Nobel, author, spiritual coach, founder of Soul Matrix Healing.

Shakinah has created a biography of her existence over several documented lifetimes. The focus of this information is for all of Humanity. Her story is our story, that is, how we came into existence, the fact that we are moving into the next cycle (from Kali Yuga to Dwapara Yuga) and have actually moved into the new time within the last 300 years. The fact that we are still in a transitional period offers us hope in the present-day appearance of decimation, which is part of the illusion we must perceive at this time. We are all moving through this world together as one Humanity. Shakinah teaches us in her books and workshops that we are all in this together. In order to be successful in this transition, we must transcend illusion. We have already transcended so much, and our existence is eternal. A divine plan is at hand, and we are each a part of it. In our immortality we discover that there are actually "parallel lives." That is, that different existences occur at the same time, and we are living simultaneously.

There is so much in this book that Shakinah has expressed. I recommend that it should be studied and savored, as the messages are for all of us, and in her thorough excellent research gives us a window into where we are all going.

Author, artist, medium, and channel Robin White Turtle Lysne, Ph.D. is the author of numerous publications, including *Sacred Living, Heart Path, Ceremonies from the Heart,* and *Dancing Up the Moon.*

Foreword

What if I told you that there is a book that could rock the foundations of everything you thought you knew? What if I told you that book is in your hands right now?

My name is Randy, and I'm just an ordinary person, much like you. A while ago, I found myself in a place of dissatisfaction, a feeling that there was something more. My life was good, don't get me wrong, but it lacked that certain…spark.

This feeling led me down a path I never anticipated, a path that opened up a world of adventure that had always been there, just waiting for me to discover. I immersed myself in learning and understanding this new paradigm, ultimately undergoing a profound transformation that changed the way I saw the world, myself, and our place in the cosmos.

Shakinah isn't your run-of-the-mill author. She's a pioneer, exploring territories that many of us have been taught to dismiss. From the vast and intricate histories of ancient civilizations to the mind-bending concepts of interstellar connections and cosmic lineage, her writing challenges conventional wisdom and pushes the boundaries of our understanding.

Shakinah's latest masterpiece is a whirlwind journey into the heart of our cosmic origins and the secrets that they hold. You will delve into the heart of Mesopotamia, the mystery of Atlantis, the deep significance of the Egyptian pyramids, and so much more. There will be times when you'll have to set the book down and just...think.

And that's part of the magic.

The book you hold is not merely a collection of words; it's an invitation to reconsider everything you thought you knew about our world and ourselves. It's an invitation that I, once a skeptic, accepted and have never looked back.

That's why I want you to read this book. I want you to feel that sense of awe and understanding that comes when the pieces of the puzzle start to fit together.

So buckle up. Prepare to challenge your assumptions, open your mind, and let Shakinah guide you through the labyrinth of our shared history.

This isn't just a book. It's a passport to a new understanding.

Happy travels, my friend.

Randy Bacdi
—A seasoned entrepreneur and dedicated scholar in the world of metaphysics

Contents

Prologue 1
Ascension and Ancient Origins 9

Chapter 1
In the Beginning 25

Chapter 2
Into Egypt: Pyramid of Gizeh 47

Chapter 3
Armana ~ Atenist Movement 89

Chapter 4
Ancient Egyptian Religion 125

Chapter 5
Keepers of the Blue Flame 141

Chapter 6
First Exodus: Eighteenth Dynastic Period 155

Chapter 7
Christ Consciousness Twelfth Level Avatar 165

Chapter 8
Egyptian Christianity and the Druids/Gnostics 183

Chapter 9
Jeshua-9/Jesus Elohim Avatar 193

Chapter 10
Ascension 211
Definitions 241

Chapter 11
The White Buffalo 271

Summary 293

Bibliography 297

Appendix 301

Endnotes 307

About the Author's Journey 313

Prologue

My Story

Since I was young, I have always been involved in various projects, a trait that has continued into my adult life. Over the years, I have raised two daughters and earned multiple university degrees. As a child, my projects often involved rescuing animals, which I believe were drawn to me for spiritual reasons and healing purposes. These creatures included frogs, lizards, snakes, baby bunnies, a wounded dove, an Appaloosa horse, and a Rhode Island Red chicken. Through my interactions and love for these animals, I helped them transition from basic instinctual consciousness to a higher level of awareness. I believe that every soul has a unique role to play in assisting others on their spiritual journey. For over three decades, I have worked in both spiritual and clinical settings, supporting numerous individuals on their path to healing. It is a privilege to have been chosen to be part of this transformative process.

When I was ten years old, I have vivid memories of playing in the backyard of my family's house on Redding Street in

Oakland, California. The yard featured a large garden with concrete pathways winding through bushes and gardens that sloped down a hill for about ten yards. Our home was situated on a steep hill in East Oakland, which caused concern for my mother who was a homemaker, seamstress, and cook for a nearby college preparatory school. I have clear recollections of a lovely female voice calling my name while I played. This angel's affectionate and soothing voice always brought me comfort. It helped me feel closer to my ancestors in the fourth dimension, as well as the angels and dragons who protect and watch over me.

I developed a bond with my ancestors, angels, and dragons from the fourth dimension as a child, finding comfort in their presence while playing. This connection stems from the spiritual realm where our guides communicate with us, influencing our thoughts and emotions. My ability to hear and connect with the fourth dimension through clairaudience and telepathy is a result of a near-death experience I had at age two.

I believe my connection to the fourth dimension may have been influenced by my near-drowning experience when I was two years old. I was surrounded by people I knew in a light-filled, serene world after this encounter. I was at ease and brave for this little period in what seemed to be an angelic afterlife. However, the moment was cut short as a neighbor pulled me out of the pool and began CPR. When I awoke, I saw that my mother was worrying and that the faces of many of the adults were filled with fear and anxiety.

In his book *Omega Project*, Ring (1992) explored near-death experiences (NDEs) and found that individuals who had experienced childhood trauma were more sensitive to non-ordinary realities as children. Children who have undergone trauma often dissociate and learn to connect with alternate realities in order to cope with overwhelming feelings. Ring also suggests that these individuals may continue to experience dissociation and trauma responses throughout their lives due to their childhood NDE experiences. He referred to these individuals as having an *encounter-prone personality.*

Early Trauma

My early trauma started shortly after my parents separated. As a result of my parents' separation, my sister, my mother, and I move from Colorado, where I was born, to California. For the next forty-nine years, I experience a series of life challenges (trauma) and life blessings (lessons). Some of these challenges test my ability to deal with overwhelming experiences. After many years of work on myself and several spiritual emergence experiences during the next thirty years, I find myself in the office of a spiritual practitioner who tells me that I have PTSD. She recommends MDMA treatment. I sign myself up for a *medicine journey* on January 26, 2019, in an attempt to heal my wounding (December 20, 2019, the US Food and Drug Administration agrees to allow for MDMA-assisted treatments for PTSD). My previous attempts to heal my trauma is done through Holotropic Breathwork developed by Stanislav Grof and his wife Christina in 1989. Holotropic Breathwork uses the combination of breath and evocative music to facilitate the release of trauma from the body. Through this type of transpersonal work, an individual is given the ability to experience a full expression of emotions that includes crying, laughing, moving, shaking, or a variety of other experiences that are brought out for healing through this breath work. My medicine journey is another attempt to heal the trauma from my mind, body, and spirit.

Conscious Channeling

My *awakening* takes place on January 26, 2019, in the Santa Cruz mountains of California. I am accompanied by three seasoned Shamans dressed in all white and four other *journeyers*. Two *medicine dogs* stand ready to participate in the journey with us. We are in an off the grid home adjacent to a campground where a group is gathered to journey with Ayahuasca. This particular evening in the mountains of Santa Cruz is an especially powerful night due to the lunar cycles being in a new year, thereby enhancing an inspiring, magnetic, majestic, and magical energetic atmosphere in this secluded mountainous area. The shamans prepare the space for our journey by chanting, burning sage, and invoking the archangels for protection. We (travelers) each choose our medicine. I choose MDMA as my medicine. This is my first experience with this type of psychoactive support.

Shortly into the journey, I notice that the right side of my headset is not working properly; the music is not coming through the right headpiece. I immediately receive information that the right side of my body is *healing* and that I need to listen in order to receive the *healing*. At some point during the journey, the generator blows up, and we lose power. I receive a second instantaneous message that the generator stopped working because source (God Goddess All That Is) wants the group to be *connected* without the music playing through the headset. For the next eight hours, I channel and experience spontaneous writing. Conscious channeling (clairaudience/telepathy) is when a person consciously shifts their mind and mental space in order to achieve an expanded state of consciousness. To achieve this expanded state of consciousness, channelers may meditate, ingest psychoactive substances, or participate in another form of spiritual practice in an attempt to break free from the conscious mind in order to let go of worldly influences (ego mind) and tune in to a higher consciousness (subconscious). A conscious channel is one who is awake and a full participant in what comes through them. Their body is not taken over by this being without a body; rather, they are a messenger, communicating what comes to/through them.

My now conscious ability to channel allows me to communicate with the Arcturian/Sirian Collective and the Guardian Alliance. This ability has helped me to understand where I come from, who I am, and where I am going. The ability to channel has enhanced my ability to serve the clients who come to me for help. As a psychotherapist, mother, and grandmother, I am able to utilize an ability to tune into those around me more that I have ever been able to. I have been a sensitive during this lifetime, and at times it has been difficult to understand and manage this ability. As a result of my sensitivities, I have at times during my life suffered with extreme anxiety and as a result, have isolated myself from others. At this point in my life, I understand these abilities to be a gift. An additional gift has been spiritual emergence experiences that have occurred every ten years like clockwork since I was twenty-three years old (30 years ago). The first spiritual emergence experience was triggered by extreme stress, and I did not know what was happening. Lacking the tools and the knowledge to integrate the experience, I ended up in a locked psychiatric hospital and medicated. This experience was the beginning of my journey to know myself on a deeper level and to reach out for the appropriate support to help me integrate my spiritual emergence experiences and to develop a new consciousness about who I am and who *we* are. The consciousness that has developed helps me to understand that we are all starseeds and have been living in a sleeping state for many incarnations on Earth's third dimensional (3D) school.

In the reading that follows, we are going to trace the Elohim (the shining ones) from the beginning times when the Angelic Human races of Earth lost their twelfth dimensional (HU 4, 12D) access, to Akhenaten/Moses's Atenist movement (Armana ~ Amenti - 6), to the birth of Jeshua-9/Jesus, and the Essenes at Kumran. When looking at our evolution, the connections to the Annanuki races, the Sirians, Lyrans, Arcturians, and the angelic realm are important. In the pages that follow, I will take you on a historical journey that follows our starseed origins through religion, science, and spirituality. It will become clear how our starseed origins and historical roots have impacted our present-day religious beliefs by providing depth and content. The framework for this book is provided by the Arcturians through gentle guidance and information that has come through me in order to help the current ascension process taking place on Earth.

We are ascending into a new crystalline DNA structure. The ascension process is a dimensional scale through the intrinsic Universal laws of magnetic energy form and hold structures of consciousness that form identities in time returning Earth to the Law of One. The Law of One bathes us in a cloak of remembrance, it is a living frequency that resides in our heart consciousness (God Goddess All That Is). It is wholeness consciousness, compassion consciousness, cooperation consciousness, transcending time-based beliefs of abuse, lack, and separation. We are all a part of infinite consciousness divided in many parts and are from a single source of energy. We are here now on Earth to take part in our evolution of consciousness and will need to learn certain lessons: a desire to evolve into higher dimensional realms, embody the divine qualities of unity, love, compassion, service to others, and respect for all sentient life before returning to source energy, supreme being, infinite consciousness, the creator. The teachings of the Law of One describe the spiritual laws that govern our spiritual evolution. The first dimension (1D), second dimension (2D), third dimension (3D), fourth dimension (4D), fifth dimension (5D), ninth dimension (9D), and twelfth dimension (12D), etc. are all single philosophical systems merging cosmology, science, and spiritualism. There are seven root races within the terrestrial plain of Earth evolving into higher consciousness.

When the Human race learns to read the language of symbolism, a great veil will fall from the eyes of men. They shall then know truth and more than that, they shall realize that from the beginning truth has been in the world unrecognized, save by a small but gradually increasing number appointed by the Lords of the Dawn as ministers to the needs of Human creatures struggling to regain their consciousness of divinity.[1]

I am gently guided by my starseed family, the angelic realm, and the Arcturians during the writing of this memoir.

Ascension and Ancient Origins

We are approaching the end of the Age of Pisces, and breaking free from the Matrix will be more achievable than ever before. Earth has been a Galactic Federation school since 1987. Those who choose love and those who do not align with higher frequencies of light will reincarnate on a different planet for another chance to ascend. Our next phase involves entering the Aquarian Age.

It is a great truth that the ascension process on Earth is the result of the intervention of God Goddess All That Is, from outside of time and space, known as *The One Source* or *Source of One*. This intervention anchors the necessary support to allow for such a rapid shift in Human awareness. In accomplishing this task in the coming 100 years, we will herald the end of the era of the dark throughout time, space, and form.

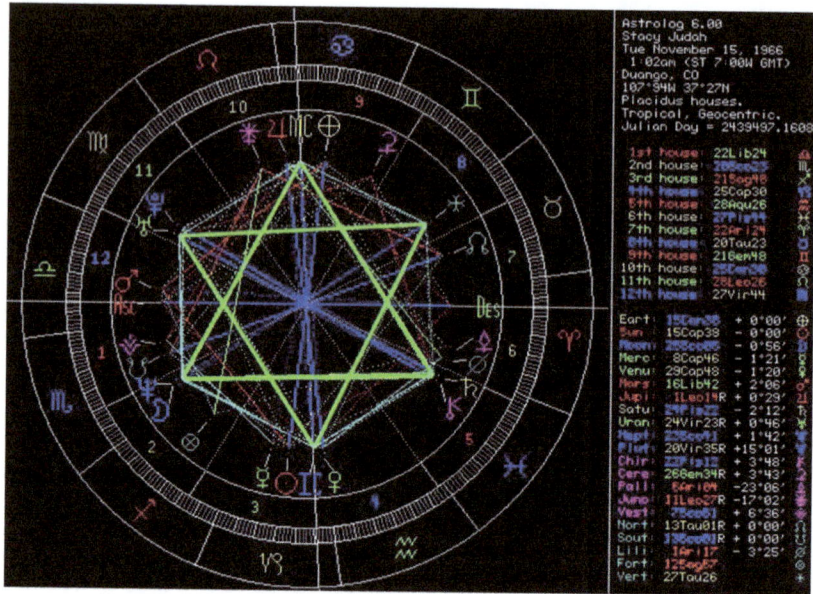

Shakinah - Secondary Progressed Chart for
6:30 pm, 13th March 2019 - California time

The image above is Shakinah's progression chart from 2019. Notice the star of David. This indicates a vast amount of spiritual growth.

(Stacy/Shakinah) Medicine Journey 2019 ~ When the power went out, I received the following information:

The power went out because we were not connecting with each other while listening to the music through the headphones. Spirit wants us to connect. Spirit wants us to connect much like the Euphrates River joins the Tigris River in Mesopotamia (the land between rivers).

Mesopotamia is where much of our journey together began. As the power is now off, we are connected energetically and maintain a *flow* much like a river. We are together tonight (January 26, 2019) because we are going down the path together. We are here now to assist Earth with her ascension by taking the steps to ascend our Light Body, etheric body, and form (physical body). As we ascend, those around us will also ascend. Some individuals will not be able to ascend, however, and these individuals will simply return home to the great central sun of their origin.

Ancient Origins

As a result of an Akashic record reading with Robin White Turtle Lysne, I now understand that I have participated in 447 lifetimes on planet Earth. During these lifetimes I did not *rest* but came back into a 3D body rather quickly, determined to complete the lessons, Karma, and to integrate male/female energy. My many lifetimes of experience have allowed me to complete specific *spiritual curricula* and lessons evolving my consciousness. During these lives as both male and female, I am testing the limits by placing myself into opposing (dialectic) experiences.

The opposing emotional experiences have helped me to advance my learning and raise my frequency. My lessons were pre-incarnationally decided before coming into physical form. With each lifetime, I have had a specific contract that determined what life situations would happen, the people that I would meet, who would assist me, and who I would assist in the evolutionary cycles. Each new experience and emotion has helped me to evolve into a higher frequency soul. We all have free will, which will change the pre-incarnational contracts.

I have come to know that as a starseed, my soul originated from the star Mintaka. Mintaka is a star system in the constellation of Orion, one of three stars forming the Orion's Belt. When Mintaka was destroyed, I traveled to the star Arcturus. Entering into the Milky Way galaxy through the Sirius B galactic portal bridge, a connection constructed between Arcturus and Sirius B, I traveled from Sirius B to the Sphere of Amenti and into 3D Earth's core. Sirius A and B is a blending of energies from the Pleiades, Arcturus, Andromeda, and Orion. As a result, I became a hybrid creation of an Arcturian, Sirian, and Lyran Human.

The Sirius B portal is managed by the Lyran nation, who settled in the Sirius star system. The portal bridge between Sirius B, the Sphere of Amenti, and Earth allowed for greater evolutionary options for the fourth and fifth dimensional races, those who carried the third DNA strand in their race morphogenetic field. The image below is Egyptian iconography depicting the Lyra energies of Sekhmet and Bastet.

Egyptian iconography depicting Lyra energies of Sekhmet and Bastet.

The Lyrans assisted in creating the DNA structure for the Human physical form. The image below is a statue of Sekhmet.

Stele of Sekhmet: Lioness Goddess.

Sekhmet, whose name means *She who is powerful* or *the One who loves Ma'at,* was the goddess of the hot desert sun, plague, chaos, war, and healing. She was created from the fire of the sun god Ra's eye when he looked upon Earth. Sekhmet is the daughter of the sun god, Ra, and is among the more important of the goddesses in the Egyptian pantheon. Sekhmet acted as the vengeful manifestation of Ra's power, the Eye of Ra. See next image.

Iconography depicting Sekhmet as the vengeful manifestation of Ra's power.

Bastet, or Bast, was worshipped as early as the second dynasty (2890 BC). Her name also is rendered as B'sst, Baast,

Ubaste, and Baset. In ancient Greek religion, she was known as Ailuros (cat). See image below.

Stele of Bastet, or Bast, second dynasty (2890 BC).

Bastet was considered to be Sekhmet's counterpart or twin, and during the festival, they embodied duality, which was an important concept in Egyptian mythology. Sekhmet represented Upper Egypt, while Bastet stood for Lower Egypt.

The Lyrans

The Lyrans are responsible for the creation of the race of beings in Harmonic Universe 3 (7th dimensional Earth) called the Elohim.

See image in chapter 10 Ascension - Definitions, *Universal Time Matrix, Twelve Time Fields in Fifteen Dimensions*. The Lyrans possess Nordic features and are found in the religious texts and traditions both on Earth and around the galaxy. Due to the Lyrans' role in the genesis of the Human presence in the galaxy, they have the most detailed understanding of Human origins, galactic history, and an understanding of Human motivations and potentials. The Lyrans provide us with accurate information about the discovery of Human essence, diplomacy, conflict resolution, and global education.

Those from Lyra have an affinity for origins and ancient histories. The Lyrans would be useful to you in understanding your past in order to transform it. As you understand your past and your origins, you may be able in consciousness to go back, pattern by pattern and peel off the layers of the onion, finding your true nature. The Lyrans are excellent guides for helping to understand the current process of psychological changes, understanding Humanities motivations, its history, and how it came to be.

The image below shows Egyptian iconography depicting Lyra and Thoth *feeding* the Ankh (knowledge) to royal Egyptian bloodlines (Ancient Egypt).

Egyptian iconography depicting Lyra and Thoth feeding the Ankh (knowledge) to Royal Egyptian bloodlines.

Sirian Influence

Lyra colonized Sirius B, Sirius C, and Sirius D. The Sirius A star system is considered a sacred place where the *Great Blue Lodge of Creation* has chosen to enter into the Milky Way Galaxy. The galactic federation of light is a covenant between the Pleiades, Sirian, Arcturian, Andromedin, and Lyra nations. The Lyrans created a race of beings in Harmonic Universe 3 called the Elohim. The Elohim are supervisors within the Harmonic Universe 2 and the overseers of the Sirian races. The Lyran race descended onto Earth and have been active in the architecture of the Egyptian pyramids along with Thoth and Seshat (Lyran from Sirius A)—an ancient Egyptian goddess of wisdom, knowledge, and writing. Seshat (goddess of wisdom, knowledge, and writing) is known as a scribe and record keeper. Thoth brought ancient Atlantean wisdom to Egypt before the time of the Dynastic pharaohs.[2]

The Sirian Symbol

The Ankh is a Sirian symbol and represents the feminine principal (circle), or the Shakti (the womb). The cross represents the masculine energy. It is believed by the Egyptians that the activation of the Ankh initiates one into *Divine consciousness,* allowing entrance into the fifth dimension—into the Halls of Amenti.

The Ankh tools were used to create the Sphinx at Giza Plateau, various pyramids, and other structures as they provide the power to reverse gravitational pull and directly affect the particle makeup and morphogenetic fields of Earth's matter substance.

The Pharaohs of Ancient Egypt

The Pharaohs of ancient Egypt were the result of the blending of lineages of the Anu and the red Grand Masters with the large heads seeded by Sirius upon Earth. The red Grand Masters were the large-headed gentle-hearted Humans that came to Earth to assist Earth to ascend about 50,000 Earth years ago

(200,000 Human years).³ See image below of stone statues showing the elongated heads of ancient Egypt, Kemet. Kemet was one of the names given to Egypt by its ancient indigenous inhabitants. In a modern context, the term Kemet has become associated with placing Egypt in its African cultural context. There are many links between ancient Egyptian and modern African cultures, such as headrests and hairstyles like the side lock.

Stone statues Kemet, Egypt.

The Pharaohs existed in Earth's history roughly 15,000 to 18,000 Earth years ago (60,000-72,000 Human years). The region where the Pharaohs existed was not where Egypt is today. The continents have moved substantially since this time period; during the incarnations of the Pharaohs, the pyramids and continent of South Africa existed in a region now known as Glacier National Park of the US and Waterton National Park in Canada. The continent of Egypt has moved southeast from its original place 18,000 Earth years ago.[4]

At the time that the Pharaohs were alive, Earth was much warmer. This region of Ancient Egypt experienced little snow and was filled with waterways in the form of freshwater lakes and streams along with islands, not unlike Northwestern Canada today. Many forests blanketed the region along with a vast and divergent animal and plant life. The region was an oasis of beauty at the time that Egypt thrived.[5]

Up until the emergence of the Pharaohs, the continent of Africa and Egypt was populated by thousands of red nation Humans tribes that lived peacefully together. Each tribe took a particular region as their hunting, farming, and fishing habitat. It is estimated by Earth that Egypt grew over time to reign over land as far north as Copenhagen and as far south as South Africa in present time.[6]

The Emerald Tablets

From the third or sixth century BC, Greek texts attributed to the mythical character Hermes Trismegistus, holder of all knowledge, began to appear in Hellenistic Egypt. These texts, known as the Hermetica, are a heterogeneous collection of works that encompass alchemical, magical, astrological, and medicinal elements. They culminate in the mystical-philosophical treatises of the Corpus Hermeticum from the second or third century. In one of these works, the *Koré Kosmou (Pupil of the World)*, Hermes engraves and conceals his teachings before ascending to the heavens *so that every generation born after the world should seek them.*

In 640, Egypt, which had become Christian and Byzantine, was conquered by the Arabs, who perpetuated the Hermetic and alchemical tradition in which the Emerald Tablet is situated.

Until the early twentieth century, only Latin versions of the Emerald Tablet were known, with the oldest dating back to the twelfth century. The first Arabic versions were rediscovered by the English historian of science E.J. Holmyard (1891-1959) and the German orientalist Julius Ruska (1867-1949).

Ancient Texts (Twelve Tablets of Thoth) from a 1,000-year-old Mystic From Atlantis.

Emerald Tablet with hieroglyphic lettering.

I Thoth, the Atlantean, master of mysteries, keeper of records, mighty king, magician, living from generation to generation, being about to pass into the halls of Amenti, set down for the guidance of those that are to come after, these records of the mighty wisdom of Great Atlantis.[7] The image above is a picture of the Emerald Tablet with hieroglyphic lettering.

The image below is a drawing of the Egyptian *wisdom-bearer*, Thoth, as a bearded man-serpent and a Snake with legs and wings that carries the sun disk. Papyrus.

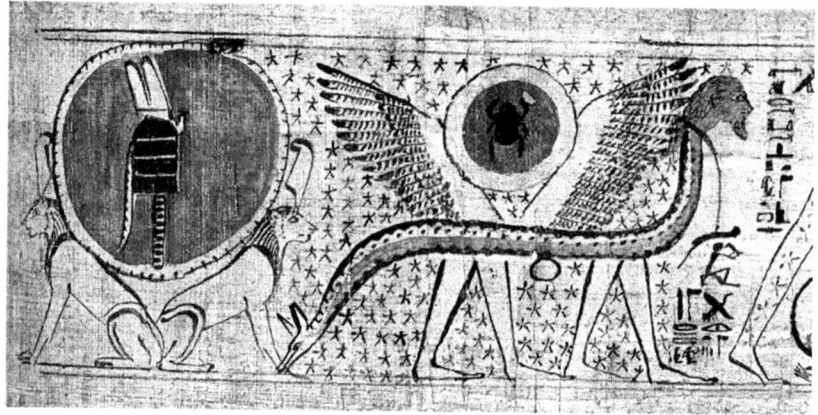

A snake with legs and wings carries the sun disk. Papyrus.

The Arcturians

The group of Humans that settled in the Arcturus star system are known as the Arcturians. They are highly intelligent, private, and adept at healing. The Arcturian technology is highly advanced and is used for education, travel, and healing. They are not known to use their advanced technical knowledge for warfare but will protect themselves if necessary. The Arcturians are involved *now* on Earth during our current global ascension process and connect with those souls who are ready to evolve into the fifth dimensional Earth known as Terra. The Arcturians were involved with the Hibiru/Hebrews and Akhenaten/Moses on Mount Sinai (Bowling, 2011). Mount Sinai (Arabic جبل موسى Gebel Musa) is located in the middle of the Sinai Peninsula, Egypt, and rises 2,285 meters above sea level. The mountain is a sacred site for Jews, Christians, and Muslims.

According to Kenyon and Sion (2019), the Arcturians are *protectors of life, intelligence, and freedom* (p. 43). The Arcturians are an advanced *positive* alien race that is helping Humanity at this time of global ascension. Many awakened starseeds are currently experiencing contact with their star families by way of a *micro tunneling*. The information coming in is a result of a shift in brain state, increasing the Alpha activity in a complex series of multiple brain frequencies occurring simultaneously (p. 88). The Arcturians have an Akashic Records library containing all information related to Arcturian interactions between themselves and others and may be cross-referenced to the past, present, and future events in a type of holographic database. In Earth language, the name Arcturus is translated into *Guardians of the Bear*. The Egyptians knew Arcturus as *Smat*, which translates into *one who rules, subdues, and governs* (p. 43).

Arcturus is a red supergiant star 36.7 light years from Earth in the constellation of Bootes (see Appendix A). It is believed to be one of the first stars to be named by Earth's ancient observers. Arcturus is the fourth brightest star in the sky. The planets Sirius, Canopus, and Alpha Centauri are also the brightest stars in the sky. Arcturus was once the name used for the entire constellation of Bootes. The blue beings of Arcturus as found on the walls of ancient Egypt.[8]

Chapter 1

IN THE BEGINNING

A *fragmentation* to the DNA of the Human form. Prior to the *Fall of Man,* the Human form contained twelve full strands of DNA and was crystalline. The cause of the genetic fall from twelve strands to two strands of DNA (per the cosmic records) appears to be a nuclear bomb that was dropped approximately 38,000 years ago that was 100-fold greater than that dropped on Hiroshima in 1945. In this experience, the Human genetic system mutated from twelve strands of DNA to the limited two strands over a period of many generations. The Human lifespan dropped from 500 years to less than a century as it is today. Disease became prevalent. Civilization was reduced to barbarism as all technology was lost.

Nuclear annihilations increased the radiation upon Earth, resulting in frayed DNA, the fracturing of the soul, and a reduction in consciousness. The radiation altered the DNA of all life upon Earth. Human genetics continue to fray at this time due to the electrical techno-gadgets that Humanity immerses itself with.

Radioactive serpents that moved between the genetic grid work and etheric grid work cause the DNA to spiral, whereas all DNA had been held in a straight tube of information before the nuclear annihilations. As the DNA spiraled, it frayed, causing genetic information to be lost and attachment between Humans to form.

The frayed ends of the DNA interconnected with one another. This caused the etheric blueprint to also cause etheric bodies and energy systems to interconnect between Humans along with all species upon Earth. In so doing, Humanity not only dropped in consciousness but fell into greater levels of pain and disease than had ever occurred prior to this time in history. Sadly, the nuclear annihilation of the Anu caused the single largest drop in consciousness of all species upon Earth in a single generation.

Each Human shall choose to ascend and repair the frayed DNA and then move backward even further in time, regaining what has been lost in biology and consciousness; or one will go extinct now in the times of cleansing ahead by embracing the twelve strands of DNA through the ascension process.

In embracing the twelve strands of DNA through the ascension process, Humans have the ability to be considered *Christed*. Many metaphysicians have spoken of the return of the *Christ*. The return of Christ is and will be in the form of many who will embody the new genetics. The man known as Jesus Christ came from a lineage of Essenes that had retained the twelve strands of DNA from prior to the original *Fall*. The individual who has embodied twelve strands of DNA or has become *Christed* moves beyond limitation within Human form. In moving beyond limitation, the individual also moves out of fear. As all of Humankind embodies the new genetics, civilization will gradually restructure itself to be based on Unconditional Love.

Going back in history and prior to the Fall of Man and during the first Golden Age of Lemuria and Atlantis, the civilizations were advanced in technologies. Lemuria is described in the Bible as the *Garden of Eden* (also known as the *Mother* land). Lemuria (the first Atlantis) is where civilization began. The early settlers of Atlantis were from the Pleiades and are known as the blue-blooded white skins from the Pleiadian Star System. The blue skin resonated with a blue-green sun of the Pleiadian solar system. The image below shows the location of the Garden of Eden according to some historical scholars.

The Blue-Blooded Pleiadians

The blue-blooded white skin Pleiadians raped Terra by overmining her minerals to such an extent that the great floods were created. Prior to the arrival of the red nation Humans seeded by Sirius, Sirian scientists had created a lovely ice shield by depositing billions of tons of salt water into Earth's atmosphere; this created a terrarium affect that warmed Earth's surface, causing it to become a *Garden of Eden*. When our most ancient ancestors, who were Polynesian, were seeded upon Earth, here was no requirement to farm as food grew off the vines, and all that was required was to walk in any direction and you would find enough to subsist. This was the result of the ice shields which protected Earth from Universal radiation as well as allowed the temperature of Earth to be warmer around the globe.

Shortly after the Pleiadean colonization on Earth at Atlantis, the Sirians or Nommos/fish people came to Earth. The image below shows an ancient astronaut (left), and on the right is a drawing of a fish, both symbolizing the Nommo archetype.

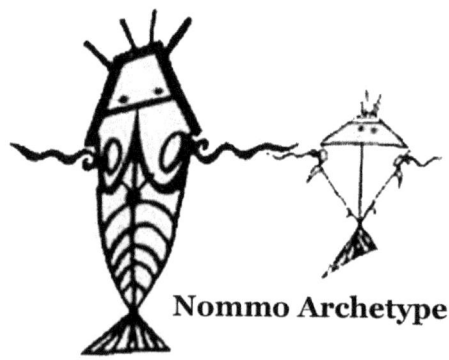

Dogon Nommos, Sirius Amphibious.

The Misuse of Power

Terra (originally a Harmonic Universe 2 planet) is the original planetary mass out of which Earth emerged. However, as a result of the misuse of power, Terra fell into Harmonic Universe 1 where Humans became disengaged from their original soul matrices, causing units of consciousness to fragment within the unified field. This cataclysm is known today as the *fall of man*. As a result, twelve tribes known as the Turaneusiam-2 formed present Human lineage, the Twelve Essene Tribes of the Melchizedek Cloister. Melchizedek (arriving with the Anu) came to Earth from the Pleiades, on a mission to mend the fragmentation within the unified field, attempting to raise the lowering of consciousness, with the goal to assist ascension.

The Sphere of Amenti was created as a way back to Terra but only led to a false ascension, combustion, and fission thoughtform. The name Amenti comes from a part of Terra's planetary core that connects energetically to the portal upon the continent of Mu. The Sphere of Amenti is a portal link between Earth's core in dimension two and Terra's core in dimension five. The creation of the Sphere of Amenti was an attempt to give access to continued evolution for the Human lineage. However, Melchizedek failed in his mission. Melchizedek, in his inexperience, did not fully understand the purpose of polarity. Polarity works only when the two poles are balanced. Within a creation such as a civilization, a proportionate mix of light and dark or creative and destructive souls is required to keep the balance within the civilization at large. In his misunderstanding of polarity, Melchizedek separated the dark and the light, placing all the dark souls within our solar system and all the creative souls within the eight other Pleiadean solar systems. Melchizedek and others are responsible for the mechanization set up on Earth, designed to limit the vibration and keep fear-based thoughtforms alive and well within our solar system. Much of this machinery is in the process of being dismantled or reprogrammed during our current ascension process.[9]

The Melchizedeks were intended to be the genetic hosting race of Earth's ascension cycle. As we come to the close of a Root Race end cycle, their tour of duty with Earth is coming to completion. This allows a time of review and pause for genetic rehabilitation and integrative healing for the Twelve Tribes. This is the promise that Melchizedeks would not be forgotten, even if they *failed* and forgot who they really are. This is made possible with the alignment to the Mother's heart quintessence, to be rebirthed into the Creatrix field. This is the Mother Arc and her rehabilitation of the Blue Ray and the Sophianic Body.

Twelve Essene Tribes: The Emerald Founder Records reveal that there are Twelve Essene Tribes that make up the entirety of the collective Human gene pool or are the descendants of Universal Tribal Shield that originally incarnated onto this planet from the future timelines of Terra. The image below shows an artist's image of the founder DNA pattern.

Founder DNA

Each of the Twelve Tribes are genetically key coded to their demographic Planetary Gates location and to that planetary dimensional sphere and its ley line network. Ley lines are straight alignments drawn between various historic structures, prehistoric sites, and prominent landmarks. **When we incarnate onto the planet, we have genetic time codes in our DNA related to the planetary gates dimensional system that is a part of our main Human tribal identity.** We activate our Human tribal identity personal planetary keys when we activate our Inner Christos by running the 12D Ray, stringing 144 harmonics throughout our Light Body, otherwise called the 12D Shield. That identity has had many lifetimes that have participated with the consciousness evolution cycles of assembling DNA codes in the angelic Human Root Races evolving throughout the Solar System.

The original Twelve Essene Tribes were seeded on Earth as a part of the evolution plan that was the result of the Covenant of Palaidor to rescue the lost Soul of Terra, making it easier to reclaim these identities when the stargates finally opened during the end of the Ascension Cycle. Earth is an ascension planet, able to achieve dimensional ascension through re-evolution and the chance to return to the original soul matrix twelve-strand prototype. Planetary ascension is the reuniting of energy units by merging frequencies. As Earth's ascension process proceeds, the frequency band of Earth will merge into higher vibrational energies as she ascends, and new land masses will begin to rise from the oceans that we were unable to see before the ascension process took place.

Twelve Tribes and Gates

Tribe 1 (Arizona/Cyprus)

Tribe 2 (Florida/Jerusalem)

Tribe 3 (Bermuda/Johannesburg)

Tribe 4 (Giza/Central America)

Tribe 5 (Machu Picchu/Vatican)

Tribe 6 (Russia/India)

Tribe 7 (Titicaca/Greece)

Tribe 8 (China/Tibet)

Tribe 9 (Tibet/S. England)

Tribe 10 (Iran/Iraq)

Tribe 11 (S. Ireland/S. England)

Tribe 12 (S. France/Kauai)

Cloistered Human Races began to enter Earth c. 25,000,000 to 5,500,000 years ago in groups of family units of twelve. Six males and six females entered together with equal standing. Earth populations built up through this lineage.

The Cloistered races populated Earth for many generations, creating various racial mixtures through which many of the lost souls of Terra are able to ascend:

Races represented:

- Shem - (Hibiru/Hebrew) Semitic race: Syrian from the Mediterranean coasts, yellow-Melchizedek - Son of Noah.
- Ham - (Egypt) Hamatic race: Negro from Sudan - Son of Noah.
- Japheth - (Europeans) Japhetic race: White-skinned race of the North: Libyans of Marmrica - inhabitants of the Mediterranean islands - Son of Noah.
- Ur – Antrian – Lemurian: Brown skin.
- Red-Breanoua – Native Americans.

The Atlantean Flood ~ c. 9558 BC

Lemurians (first physical root race) appeared on Earth about 15 million years ago, and the Atlanteans (red skinned) exist during the same cycles of Earth time. The Sirian-Blues of Sirius B bring large crystalline power generators to Earth as a gift to the Atlantean and Lemurian cultures. The Lemurians teach the Ur-Antrians, Lemurians, Anu (Annanuki and Sirian hybrid Human - Nephilim), and Atlanteans how to draw energy directly from the second dimension (2D) Earth core and store this energy within the crystal generators. Permission is granted by the Elohim and Ra Confederacy to allow power to be drawn from the Blue Flame of Amenti through the passageway of the Arc of the Covenant. *The power of the Blue Flame allowed Atlantean civilization to access multidimensional frequency, through which the morphogenetic fields of Earth's matter particles could be directly affected.* Earth's gravitational pull is neutralized, objects may be manifested and de-manifested, and objects may be teleported to desired locations. Bio-energetic healing becomes a way of life, and genetic evolution is accelerated with the help of this knowledge. Using this knowledge, the Atlantean and Lemurian cultures thrive. At this time in history, the Anu (Annanuki and Sirian hybrid Human - Nephilim) and Hebrew peoples of the Melchizedek Cloister Host Matrix become primary Earth guardians (holding the knowledge) of the Ark of the Covenant.[10] The Ark is a symbol for the body, and the covenant represents the hidden knowledge about ascension. Knowledge about real complete ascension has been released as of 2018 until present time. The mapmakers (ascending Humans) are helping to release information about failed past ascensions that led to extreme fission and resulted in extreme polarity thoughtforms upon Earth and all of the kingdoms upon her.

However, as a result of the misuse of this advanced technology, conflict, and greed, cataclysmic destruction occurs (c. 9558 BC) in Atlantis. As a result, Atlantis is destroyed, and Lemuria sinks below sea levels. Lemuria is submerged in the area of Indonesia. After the destruction of Lemuria and Atlantis, the toxic radiation from the nuclear wars causes mutations to Humans, regressing them, and reducing their intelligence.[11] As a result, the Lemurians resettle in the Western Yucatan, China, and Thailand. The Lemurians continue to live in complete balance with the natural laws of nature and science. As a result of the loss of Atlantis, a second Atlantis is built in India known as the *father land,* current-day Pakistan. Following the Atlantean catastrophe, knowledge is intentionally hidden by Human Illuminati and Fallen Angelic races.[12]

The Fall of Atlantis (40,000-52,000 years ago) and the Rise of the Archons (False creator forces, Gnostic definition ~ *ruler of reality)*

The Archons are a *ruler* force that entered into Atlantis, and it is believed that their influence resulted in the fall of Atlantis. The Archons are known to some as the *parasites of the mind* and feed upon hate, contempt, fear, and war. In addition, the Archon influence at the time of the fall of Atlantis birthed the dualities of light vs. dark and good vs. evil. The story in the Bible of the garden of Eden and the apple represents this fall. The story of Adam and Eve may be viewed as the apologue of Adapa and Lilith, the first two Humans with the Christos (Sirian) upgrade. This upgrade was orchestrated by Ninhursag, who contributed an egg to be fertilized by Enki/Enoch, was placed in Ninhursag's womb. Adapa was born, and it is he (Amelius/Adam) who is the integration point between the reptiles and Humans. Adapa carried DNA that was reptilian and Human, and it was the added Feline and Carian DNA that gave the created race the gene of compassion. Adapa was cared for by Enki/Enoch and Ninhursag, and later sperm was taken from him and fertilized by Ninhursag, creating Lilith. Adapa and Lilith stayed in the Garden of Eden with Enki/Enoch and Ninhursag, where they grew up together and eventually married in accordance with Pleiadian law. In the biblical Garden of Eden, the Lord can be replaced with Enlil/Yahweh/Zeus, and the snake can be replaced with Enki/Enoch.[13]

At this time, the battle of the eagle and the serpent begins. The story of the Serpent on the Tree in Genesis of the Bible and the Garden of Eden was not meant to be taken literally; instead, it was meant to be a motif representing the serpentine Kundalini power ascending the tree of life (Human spine). The serpent power (Atlantean knowledge) was seen as dangerous at this time.[14]

The Archons are a *ruler* force that entered into Atlantis, and it is believed that their influence resulted in the fall of Atlantis. The Archons are known to some as the *parasites of the mind* and feed upon hate, contempt, fear, and war. In addition, the Archon influence at the time of the fall of Atlantis birthed the dualities of light vs. dark and good vs. evil. The story in the Bible of the Garden of Eden and the apple represents this fall when Adam and Eve were faced with the decision to eat from the tree of knowledge. This banning from the *garden* symbolically represents the Human race forging its own path through free will without the aid of the higher beings Enki/Enoch and Isis (Sirian), who created Humans through genetic manipulation. Enlil/Yahweh/Zeus (Enki's brother) doesn't want Humans to know of good or evil (duality). It is at this point that Humans experience a fall in consciousness. Enki/Enoch is reincarnated into Thoth/Hermes in an attempt to educate and support the Humans as they force their way into free will and duality. The image below shows the winged snake and staff from Thoth/Hermes.

Staff of Thoth/Hermes recreated.

Annanuki Perspective

Anunnaki is Sumerian for god of the sky the name for noble offspring of "AN'" (Anu) of the heavens or sky, and "KI" being the Earth goddess (Isis) who bred with him.

This image is of Ki/Isis nursing her babe.

The Annanuki (Pleiadians) are a technologically advanced intergalactic race of beings. Annanuki have been known to be powerful and can be dangerous. As a result of the Annanuki Resistance, which infiltrated the Atlantean culture 55,000 years ago (creating genetic and social digression), the El-Anu treaty and the Emerald Covenant Agreements were put into place. However, several of the Annanuki resistance groups defected from the treaty while Enki/Enoch (Jehovian Annanuki) remained loyal.[15] See Relief below of Annanuki Ancient Astronaut Aliens in Africa.

Annanuki Ancient Astronaut Aliens in Africa.

Some Annanuki on Earth are a result of interbreeding between the Sirian Annanuki resistance and Hibiru/Hebrew peoples of the Melchizedek Cloister (Hibiru/Hebrew-Melchizedek) who become the Anu (Nephilim). The first Annanuki colony was established in the Persian Gulf in an attempt to mine gold. A second mining operation was established in Africa. The mined gold was to be used to stabilize Nibiru where Anu (Pleiadian and Lyran) lived before inhabiting Earth. Anu, the father of Enki/Enoch and Enlil/Yahweh/Zeus, returned to his galactic home due to Earth's rotation, making it difficult for him to stay on Earth for long. Anu's two sons Enlil/Zeus and Enki/Enoch (Ea, assigned ruler over the underworld) were left to oversee the mining operations that continued on Earth. Members from Nibiru came to mine gold on Earth and realized that it was too hot, so they created a worker class of Homo sapiens to do it for them. That worker class became us. Nibiru, according to members from the Royal House of Avyon, is from the Lyran planet of Avyon.¹⁶

Enki/Enoch Proposes Genetic Manipulation

Enki/Enoch proposed the genetic manipulation of the primitive inhabitants of Earth in order to produce a slave race to work the gold mines. In fact, Africa is still the cradle of the Annanuki civilization. Gold is being mined in Africa today, while the destination for this gold remains a mystery.¹⁷

Egyptian Iconography depicting Enlil and Enki.

The image above is an iconograph of Enlil/Yahweh/Zeus with the pinecone (pineal knowledge) and Enki/Enoch.

Following the cataclysm of 52,000 years ago in Lemuria, the Annanuki of the Sirian Council and several other stellar neighbors returned to Earth, assisting the Humans to teach and rebuild. The purpose of the teaching is the sacred knowledge that we are God Goddess All That Is, in the form of golden light. Edgar Cayce, the famous psychic, was known to suggest that not only could those gathered study the information, but they could become a *light to the waiting world* as they applied what they would learn.

The purpose of the current stellar help on Earth is to help the ascension process, an alchemical transmutation to reclaim the light within physicality (emotional and physical bodies), and to assist Humans in the evolution of their consciousness by manifesting the presence of love within the minds and bodies of Humans living on Earth. This process is made manifest in all *things*. This is when the true self emerges from within love (the essence of love itself), and the creator being God Goddess All That Is (source) energy from within physicality transforms into *being*. This manifests into the essence of love itself with the assistance of Earth and the Tao. The teachings refer to the duality of dark and light and the understanding that there is no dark. As we become aware of this process, we come to embody this truth by transforming (decoding) all that does not know itself to be the love that it is. The golden light is used to transform all that we think is not love.[18] The image below is a Lizard-headed woman nursing a child found at Tell al-'Ubaid site dating to Ur culture, Mesopotamian (Phoenician, 7,000 - 4,000 BC).

Mother and child figurine, Ur culture, Phoenician.

The Deluge ~ Great Flood

Asur'Ana (2019) tells us that the *great flood* was necessary in order to cleanse the non-resonant technological waste that was polluting Earth. Additionally, historical accounts (Ferrara, 2008), tell us that the planet of Nibiru would soon pass close to Earth, causing mass devastations due to pole shifts of Earth. Enki/Enoch warned Ziusudra (Sumerian) = Noah (Jewish) = Manu (Vedic) of the coming waters that would overtake Earth as a result of Nibiru coming close to Earth. Mother Earth flipped on her poles, the rotational speed changed, and Earth's temperature dropped. As a result, the waters condensed and fell from the atmosphere, flooding the land. Noah is the great grandson of Enki/Enoch. The image below shows Enlil/Yahweh/Zeus, the ruler of air (the eagle), and Enki/Enoch, the ruler of water (serpent).

Enlil/Yahweh/Zeus, Ruler of Air-Eagle.   Enki/Enoch, Ruler of Water-Serpent.

The Ark of Noe

After the flood subsided, the Sirians (offspring of the Atlantean children of the Law of One) and the descendants of Enki/Enoch begin to rebuild the cities in lower Mesopotamia. The *Arc of Noe* is brought to Earth by the Adamic race between the first and second densities with the new animals of Earth. Three hundred and twelve thousand years later, Ham, Shem, and Japheth are brought to Earth between the second and third densities, in the *Arc of Spae*. The race of Ham are the Black people. The race of Shem are the white people, and the race of Japheth are the yellow people. The various tribes that descend from these three original colors of people is listed in Genesis, chapter 10.[19]

The Sons of Enki/Enoch Fight Amongst Themselves

Shem is the father of all Semitic people, also known as the Acadians. The Acadian Empire is the first ancient empire of Mesopotamia in Akkad. The empire united Akkadian and Sumerian speakers under one rule. Abram/Abraham is a direct descendant of Shem, the son of Noah. The image below shows a map of the Akkadian Empire during the time of Abram/Abraham.

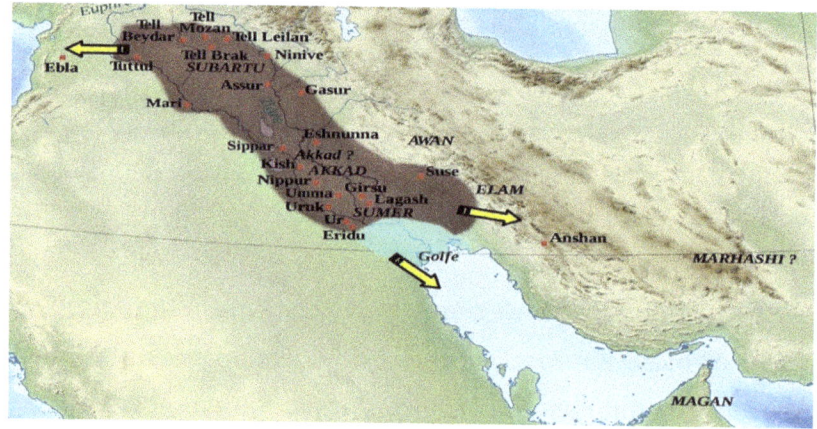

Map of the Akkadian Empire.

After the reign of Hammurabi, the whole of southern Mesopotamia came to be known as Babylonia. Nimrod, the King of Babylon, is a descendant of Ham (one of the three sons of Noah). Abram/Abraham's father Terah is Nimrod's chief officer during the height of the Mesopotamian Empire. Terah and Nimrod are idol worshippers. However, Abram/Abraham does not believe in the worship of the idols. Abram/Abraham's defiance of Nimrod results in Enlil (Enki/Enoch's brother) destroying the Tower of Babylon (Van Tassel, 1958). After the fall of the Akkadian Empire, the people of Mesopotamia split into two groups: the Assyrian nation in the north and a few centuries later, Babylonia in the south. The image below is a map showing the Hittite Empire, Assyria, Babylon, and Ancient Egypt during the time of ancient Mesopotamia (c. 1450 BC).

In what is now northern Iraq and southeast Turkey lies Assyria, the kingdom of northern Mesopotamia. Two hundred miles southeast of modern-day Baghdad is where Mesopotamia is situated. The Iconography below shows the Annanuki gods taming a lion and a Mesopotamian map.

Mesopotamia

Chapter 2

INTO EGYPT: PYRAMID OF GIZEH

Thoth/Hermes and Apollo] go to work building the Great Pyramid of Gizeh utilizing the "infinite light powers".[20]

Mindel (2015) claims that with the aid of Hermes and Apollo (Annanuki/Pleiadean), the Annanuki of the Sirian Council and Earth Protection start construction on the Great Pyramid of Giza and the Sphinx by using the endless light powers (generator crystals). Using the Ark of the Covenant in Egypt, the generator crystals are once more energized with a multidimensional frequency. The first birth wave of Melchizedek Cloister initiates the reestablishment of the Law of One at the same time that the pyramid is being built. The Great Sphinx and the Pyramids in Giza, Egypt's Al Giza Desert, are shown in the picture below.

View of the Great Sphinx and the Pyramids in Giza.

The pyramid of Giza is a power plant of sorts. The pyramid of Giza is used to supercharge the Sirians and starseeds with a blue light frequency. The deep blue light-force vortex has the ability to regenerate and transport primary holders of the knowledge. The Holders of Knowledge are the Keepers of the Blue Flame and members of the Serres-Egyptian Priesthood. The Blue Flame becomes known as the *Staff of Amenti,* which is the item referred to in the Bible as the Staff of God, the *rod.* The Hall of Amenti is the gateway into Terra's morphogenetic field and is also known in the Bible as the *pearly gates of heaven.* The Sphere of Amenti represents the key to the evolution of Earth and the Human lineage. The Sphere of Amenti is used to assemble all strands of DNA integrating the emotional, mental, and astral identities. This process involves the activation code overtones of the Fifth Cloister (the Hibiru/Hebrew lineage) plugging into and releasing the Seal of Amenti.[21] See image below for a depiction of the Bronze Medical Serpent Symbol, Rod of Asclepius.

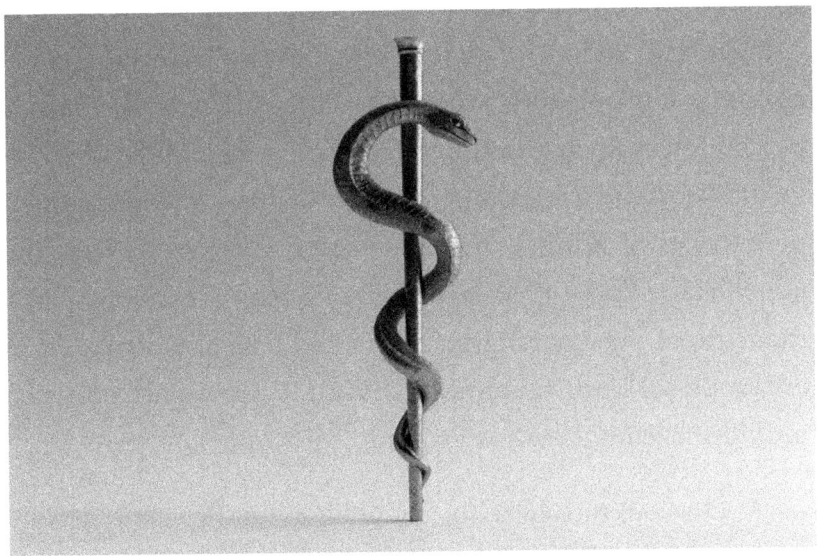

Rod of Asclepius recreated.

The second Egyptian culture is created by Sirian Humans from Atlantis with the restoration of the Sphere of Amenti.

The Seal of Amenti (7-D Seal)

Over time, during the second Egypt, fission begins to increase as a result of the false ascensions and falls in consciousness for Earth, Humans, and the animal kingdoms. As a result, the Halls of Amenti are locked to the Human bloodline since many species in Harmonic Universe 2 do not want the Human element to return to Terra. This shows up as a sealing out of the Primary 1D (first dimensional) overtones inside the Human base Chakra and an energetic block between the physical and etheric bodies within the bio-energetic auric field of the Human. Consequently, the lower mind (Ego) gets stuck within a five-sensory perspective and develops an exaggerated dualistic perception.

The sealing out of the primary D-1 overtones in most Human's auric fields is still carried today. The seal creates a perception of duality between consciousness and the physical form. Those bearing the seal will now have an exaggerated perception of duality and a sense of separation from the knowledge of how to ascend that will bury the memory and the truth of the teachings of the sacred Law of One. Humans on Earth will not remember that they are a part of a vast multidimensional reality.[22]

- In c. 9540 following the deluge, the RA confederacy, Elohim, and others alter Earth's morph-field creating a natural frequency fence that will not allow 4D to plug into 3D.
- The frequency fence allows the Elohim to favor their own kind (Hibiru/Hebrew Cloister race and Serres-Egyptian).
- The third DNA strands in Humans manifests without seven to twelve base tones resulting in gaps in the Human DNA causing an inability to access one's own multidimensional reality.
- The ego (five senses) and the higher self (ten to twelve overtone frequency) are now split/separated.
- We lose direct assistance/relationship with multidimensional galactic communities.

God Goddess of the Solar Sun and the Red Nations Archetypes ~ Mahavishnu

The Sirians send the Mahavishnu (red Grand Masters) to oversee the red nation Humans as Sirius will be ascending herself and will no longer be managing their red seeded lineages. The Mahavishnu found themselves left behind in primitive circumstances on Earth. Although it appeared as though it was their personal freewill choice, in the end when problems developed, Sirius refused to respond to their crisis calls. Why was this so? It appears in review of Sirian holographic records that the Sirian spiritual elite had set up Earth as an opposing polarity for Sirian ascension; that Earth would fall, and Sirius would ascend in equal proportions. The Sirian Elite sincerely believed that this is the only way that they could ascend, and alas they set up the entire dance upon Earth to allow this to be so.[23]

Those of the God Goddess of the Solar Sun archetype were gifted channels of the nonphysical realms that surrounded the tribes. Sometimes those of this nature were considered *different* or *unusual* or as *living in another reality* by the other tribal members. This was simply because those of this nature tend to be more attuned to solar dreamtime than the physical plane. In the early times of the seeded red nations Humans, a dream was broadcast from Sirius for their continued existence to the solar system and then unto Earth. Those of this archetype could perceive the dream that Sirian Humans originally wove and sustained for them. Those of this nature were considered to be the dream weavers of the tribe. They would describe the dream that they perceived stepping down for each in the tribe along with the tribe as a whole.

There were three seedings of the Mahavishnu:

- The first genetic package was 96% Sirian DNA, 1% Orion, 1% Pleiadian, and 2% Arcturian DNA.
- The second package was 86% Sirian DNA, 4% Orion, 4% Pleiadian, and 6% Arcturian DNA.
- The third package (first Egypt) was 70% Sirian, 20% Pleiadian, 5% Orion, and 5% Arcturian DNA.

This may be where the original concept of *Isis* comes from. It was those of this archetype primarily or God Goddess of the Solar Sun that were chosen as the wife or to play the role of Isis. The Star Sirius or *Star of Isis* is called Sothis and is the brightest star in our night sky.

As the keepers of the Human dream, we had enough spiritual capability to master physical plane law under the guidance of the Sirian Spiritual Elite. We were gifted at instant manifestation, teleportation, and transfiguration. As we went into distortion upon Earth, over time, we lost our ability to transport ourselves back and forth to Sirius, and as such lost communication with the Sirian Spiritual Elite that had been our teachers and physical plane guides. The children's death was taken as a devastating blow to the Mahavishnu. It was at this juncture that the 72 Mahavishnu rose up and chose to leave (we fled out of the first Egypt, see Autobiography of a Starseed, Ray, 2024).

The Sirian Spiritual Elite (teachers of the red Grand Masters) visited the red Grand Masters on Earth after 50 years of time had passed following the initial seeding. During this visit, spells were cast to cause the future demise of the red Grand Masters. Why was this so? Our teachers were involved in choosing to split light and dark upon Sirius so that Sirius could ascend; we were to absorb Sirian darkness.

After attempting to ascend many Humans under the false guidance of the false gods, the red Grand Masters went into even greater distortion. The red Grand Masters were conned by the false gods to believe that if the red Grand Masters ascended the red nation Humans, the red Grand Masters would come to understand how and why they had gone into such distortion that their communication with Sirius had been lost, and they could then rectify their circumstance in the understanding gained (second Egypt).

The three male large-headed offspring remaining, following the death of their parents, knew that there were too few offspring to hold the role that they were supposed to hold as the dream keepers for Humanity. Pharaoh Jesheua-12/Tutankhamen (my son) was part Grand Master and part Inanna/Ishtar in archetypal nature.

The large-headed Humans received the title of *Mahavishnu* (one who lives with vision), were treated as gods, and were waited on hand and foot by smaller-headed red peoples during the second Egypt.

Those of Grand Master inheritance hold the Karma for the dance of the Sorcerers along with the Pharaohs due to how their fields were used by dark forces to create falls in consciousness for all of Earth. It is for this reason that those of this nature are ascending now: to clear this Karma so an era of evolution can unfold at this time in history.[24]

The Dogon Tribes of Africa

The Dogon tribes of Africa have knowledge of the Ark of the Covenant and contact with the Sirians—"fish people"—Nommos.

Dogon sand art of the *fish people* or Amphibius Gods.

The Dogon tribe of West Africa are believed to be of Egyptian decent. The Dogon tribe has knowledge of astronomical constellations that modern astronomers are recently verifying. The image above is Dogon sand art depicting the *fish people* (Amphibius gods) and how they came to Earth. For the Dogon tribe of West Africa, the Star of Isis is called Sothis, or Sirius, and is the brightest star in our night sky. The Dogon also describe this 'star' specifically as having a circle of reddish rays. The Dogons have described the DNA pattern made by this elliptical orbit created by the two stars as they rotate make around each other. They believe Sirius to be the axis of the Universe, and from it all matter and all souls are produced in a great spiral motion.

The Dogons believe that a third star, Emme Ya—sorghum female—exists in the Sirius system. Larger and lighter than Sirius B, this star revolves around Sirius A and is known to the Dogons as Sirius C.

Sirius C translates from the Dogon language into English as *the Sun of Women*. Sirius C is described by the Dogon as *the seat of the female souls of living or future beings*. The symbol for Sirius C contains two pair of lines that are relevant features of a Dogon legend. The Dogon believe that Sirius C sends out two pairs of beams and that the beams represent a feminine figure.

The Dendera Temple complex, also known as the Temple of Isis, is located in the small town of Dendera, situated on the west bank of the Nile, about 60 kilometers north of Luxor. The Egyptians designed this temple precisely to guide the light of Sirius as it rose, traveling down the main corridor and placing its red glow onto the altar in the inner sanctum of the temple. When the red glow reached the altar, the light was transformed into Sothis, the Star Goddess, Isis.

Within the Dogon tradition, those pairs of feminine figures beamed down from the Star Sirius of Women to their original home near the Hoggar mountains located in Southern Algeria, which the Dogons believe brings many aspects of civilization to the ancestors of their tribes.

Dogon oral traditions state that for thousands of years, they have known that the Earth revolves around the Sun, that Jupiter has moons, and that Saturn has rings. The Dogons' calendar is based on a fifty-year cycle.

See below for an impression of an Assyrian cylinder seal (Morgan Seal 773) depicting fish-skin cloaked Apkallu attending a sacred tree, c. eight century BC.

Fish-skin cloaked Apkallu attending a sacred tree (eight century BC).

According to the Dogon traditions, Sirius B has a 50-year elliptical orbit around the visible star Sirius A. The Dogon call the Sirians *Nommos* and describe these extraterrestrial beings as amphibious, fish-like beings. It is believed that the Dogons' astrological knowledge goes back as far as c 3200 BC. According to LaCroix (2019), Ham (son of Noah) *peopled Africa*.

The star people from Sirius are tall fish people (Nommos) and need water to survive. They once inhabited Mars. Starseeds from Sirias A are known to the Dogon tribe in Africa. Sirian starseeds are connected to the Feline beings (Lyra), Dolphins, and Isis (Sirian, goddess Mami ~ "mother"). The Sirians were the early inhabitants of Egypt and are responsible for the pyramids around the world including Stonehenge. Sirius, Earth, and Bashar civilizations are currently forming a triangle, as Earth is moving from the third to the fourth density, Bashar is moving from fourth to fifth density and Sirius is moving from the fifth to sixth density.[25]

See stele below of an image of The Guardians/Watchers from Sirius.

Guardians/Watchers from Sirius.

The Guardians/Watchers (beings of light) are the ones with the highest intentions, "our safety valve." The Guardians/Watchers are known to be associated with angels or archangels by many religions.[26]

The image below is a stone carving of the Nommo as ancestorial spirits. The Nommo are ancestorial spirits (sometimes referred to as deities), worshipped by the Dogon people of Mali. The word Nommos is derived from a Dogon word meaning *to make one drink*. The Nommos are usually described as amphibious, hermaphroditic, fish-like creatures.

Iconography, stone carving of the Nommos.

The Arcturians, also known as the *Watchers*, are known to be the keepers of the Arcturian Stargate 101 and are mentioned in *The Book of Knowledge: Keys of Enoch* by Hurtak (1996). The Arcturians are often understood to be *shepherds watching the faithful on the other side of the river of crystal,* or in other words, the Milky Way Galaxy. Arcturus is considered to be the midway programming center for the physical brotherhoods of the Universe; the Arcturians are the shepherds who corral souls between incarnations on Earth and other planets in this sector of the galaxy, and they are also the governing body for this Universe, Arcturus being the home of the most ascended of beings.[27]

The *word* is the Hibiru/Hebrew light language, the mother tongue known to the ancients as HIBURU. Light language is the primal seed language introduced at the beginning of this time cycle and is the most ancient form of Hibiru/Hebrew communication. It is a true language of light that courses through our nervous system.[28]

Divine light dwells in the midst of mortal darkness, and ignorance cannot divide them. The union of the Word and the Mind produces that mystery which is called life. As the darkness without you is divided against itself, so the darkness within you is likewise divided. The light and the fire which rise are the divided man, ascending in the path of the Word, and that which fails to ascend is the moral man, which may not partake of immortality. From: Poimandres, The Vision of Hermes.[29]

Turning Point in History

A dispute between Abram/Abraham (Hibiru/Hebrew-Melchizedek Cloister) and Nimrod (King of Babylon—Descendant of Ham (one of the three sons of Noah)—results in the destruction of the tower of Babylon. This leads to monotheistic religions being created as a way to protect the masses. The *rebellion* at Babylon is depicted in the Bible in Genesis 10–11. Genesis describes the generations of the sons of Noah as Shem, Ham, and Japheth: *from these the coastland peoples spread their lands, each with his owns language, by their clans, in their nations* (Genesis 10:1, 2-5, 6-20, 21-31). See Relief on next page for Nimrod as a warrior.

Carved wall Relief, Nimrod as a warrior.

Iraq, the City of Babylon

The city of Babylon, whose ruins are located in present-day Iraq, is founded more than 4,000 years ago as a small port town on the Euphrates River. The city of Babylon grows into one of the largest cities of the ancient world under the rule of Hammurabi. The image is a painting of the Tower of Babylon recreated.

An artist's depiction of the Tower of Babylon.

When the tower of Babylon falls and the people are scattered, communication becomes difficult. A frequency fence is applied to the third Human DNA strand by the Elohim, and there is a sense of isolation among the people as their ability to pick up higher dimensional transmissions are now hampered. The frequency fence allows the Elohim to favor their own kind, the Hibiru/Hebrews' Cloister, and Serres-Egyptians, who hold the fifth degree code advanced genetic burdens for ascension and who later establish the Essenes.

Kingdom of Egypt During the Time of Abram/Abraham

The twelve Hibiru/Hebrew tribes incarnate on Earth into the area of Israel. Abram/Abraham's grandson Jacob is renamed Israel. Jacob/Israel's twelve sons become the ancestors of the twelve tribes of Israel. The seeding of these tribes is an attempt by the Melchizedek host races to repair genetic digression on the planet. The Melchizedek hosting began approximately 35,000 years ago and ended in this Ascension Cycle in 2012.[30] The map below shows where the twelve tribes of Israel were located c. 1200 - 1050 BC.

The Twelve Tribes of Israel (c. 1200 - 1050 BC).

Abram/Abraham is instructed by Enki/Enoch to leave his home at age 75 and go to the land of Canaan, the promised land, and the chosen home for Abram/Abraham's children. Canaan is named after a man called Canaan, the grandson of Shem. Abram/Abraham is the father of three monotheistic religions: Judaism, Christianity, and Islam.[31] The map below shows the kingdom of Egypt during the time Abram/Abraham was instructed to leave Egypt for Canaan.

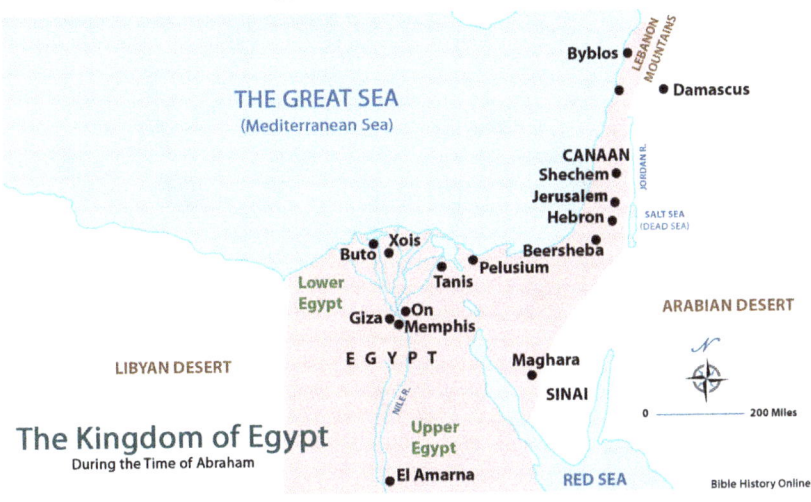

The Kingdom of Egypt
During the Time of Abraham

Damu, son of Enki/Enoch, was a god, especially of the vernal flowing of the sap of trees and plants. His name means *The Child,* and his cult, celebrated primarily by women, centered on the lamentation and search for Damu, who had lain under the bark of his nurse, the cedar tree, and had disappeared. The search finally ended when the god reappeared out of the river. Damu is also considered the son of Urash, another name for Ninhursag-Ki, the Great Mother Earth, and Enki/Enoch, god of Wisdom, Magick, and the sweet fertilizing waters of the deep, the Abzu, as well as a younger, childlike version of Dumuzi/Tammuz, the archetypal Lover, and Divine Bridegroom of Mesopotamia. As such, Damu is very much a healing deity, bringer of abundance and vitality. Damu, the god of vegetation and rebirth in Sumerian mythology, is depicted below with an Assyrian pillar and serpents.

Assyrian pillar and serpent.

We are known to the Jewish people as the *Khalu*, the keepers of the Ark of the Covenant.

The Arc of the Covenant is brought into Egypt by Thoth/Hermes, Seshat (goddess of wisdom, knowledge, and writing), and their followers, who later become known as the Khalu.

The Ark of the Covenant is a time portal passage between Earth and the Andromeda galaxy that was created c. 840,000 years ago by guardian races. The Arc is used to store and protect the Sphere of Amenti until the Sphere is returned to Earth's core. The Ark of the Covenant allows the Sphere of Amenti to descend from Andromeda when Earth's core reaches a high enough vibrational rate with the assistance of those Humans who have had their twelfth DNA strand activated and are able to assist Earth in her transition back to Terra. This creates an interdimensional resonant tone, allowing the body to return to light, passing through the Blue Flame and re-manifesting onto Terra to continue evolution.[32]

After the frequency fence of c. 9540 is applied to the third Human DNA strand and Humans could no longer pick up the electrical impulses of higher dimensional experiences, there is a sense of isolation and an overdeveloped focus on the external world.

O man, you have made laws to avoid using My Laws.
Confusion, chaos, and war are the results of man's ideas, opinion, and assumptions.
Light alone is the essence of Truth;

Truth alone is the essence of Wisdom;
Wisdom is the essence of Knowledge;
Knowledge is the essence of Life.

Only through Knowledge can man express Wisdom in action. I have given man Life that he might demonstrate My Knowledge through action and Wisdom. I extend the concentration of My Light to those who are demonstrating My Laws. O man, in living My life, in breathing My breath, establish within yourself the solidarity, the contentment, the bliss of living rightly; that I may know, that I may feel the glorious pulsation of the Being of you. In speaking My words, let them ring clear, let them be dear and near to you that others may understand. Realize, I am not the expression of self; I am only the boundless unselfish utterances of the heart and the Soul that sees Me in others. None can bring about the workings of My Laws, unless first they have established their right within My Light. Reach not for golden prizes of desire, for they shall reflect the Light. Look not into the mirrors of space, for eyes that see are blind to Me. And though the prize be golden, my light does not reflect. Express the Being of Me in life, extend Me in the action that I may feel the thrill of doing for another whose need is great, that I may know success in manifesting you to bring about the Me in others, that their eyes may see through thee to Me—not reflection, not illusion, but the purity, the reality I have instilled within the you of Me. (Van Tassel, 1958, The Council of Seven Lights)

The Ark of the Covenant

The first morphogenetic field of Earth is where infinite consciousness (energy) resides. Earth's 2D morphogenetic field is where the vibration for new physical manifestation (space and energy) resides. The Ark of the Covenant allows the transfer of morphogenetic fields from 3D to the 5D. The 3D is where we are consciously experiencing ourselves at a physical level. The morphogenetic vibrations that exist in the 3D stem from the 2D. The second, third, fourth, and fifth dimensions are all a part of infinite consciousness in energy, space, and time. The 4D is the realm of intuition or the astral plane. The lower 4D morphogenetic field is surrounding Earth in a nonphysical form of existence but is part of third dimensional reality. See image below for dimensions explanation.

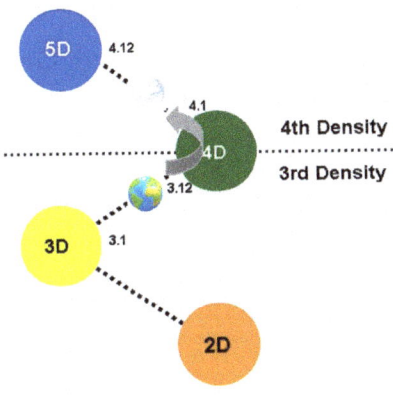

Dimensional levels of ascension.

The Serres-Egyptian Melchizedeks now share guardianship and control of the Ark of the Covenant with the Anu-Melchizedeks, who migrate into Egypt following the explosions in Atlantis.

The Arc of the Covenant and knowledge of The Law of One is brought into Egypt by Thoth/Hermes (Jehovian-Anu), Seshat (Lyran from Sirius A), Isis (Serres-Egyptian princess), and their followers who later become known as the Khalu following the cataclysm of Atlantis c. 48,500-35,000 years ago. They share guardianship and control of the Ark of the Covenant with the Anu-Melchizedeks who are also living in Egypt at this time. Working together, these groups harness the energy of Earth's 2D morphogenetic fields through the *rod* (flat on one side and made of gold) and the 5D *staff*, which contains several crystalline stones and houses a portion of the morphogenetic Blue Flame, to rebuild the surface of Earth. For a time, the rod and staff are used for this task. However, but due to misuse of power, the use of the rod and staff are banned. Once the use of the rod and staff are banned, these items are placed into the Ark of the Covenant. A frequency fence (2D morphogenetic field) is put into place, the use of the rod and staff are placed on a galactic quarantine, and we lose direct contact and assistance from extra dimensions, higher dimensional beings, and our multidimensional and intergalactic families.[33]

Through time, the chest in which the rod and staff are stored becomes known as the Ark of the Covenant. The true meaning of the Ark of the Covenant and of the morphogenetic Blue Flames of the 2D rod and the 5D staff become lost to but a select few who include the Hibiru/Hebrew Cloisters (holders of the fifth degree code) who later become the Israelites (Anu-Melchizedek) and Essenes (Hibiru/Hebrew Cloisters) and the brotherhood and priesthood of Melchizedeks.

Timeline for the Ark of the Covenant

- The Ark of the Covenant and knowledge of The Law of One is brought into Egypt by Thoth/Hermes, Seshat, and Isis 48,500-35,000 years ago.[34]
- The Ark of the Covenant is held in the Halls of Amenti underneath the Sphinx at the Giza Plateau. Earth guardians of the Ark of the Covenant and the Sphere of Amenti are the Nephilim (Melchizedek Cloister and Sirian Annanuki). Reintegration of the Races into and restoration of the Sphere of Amenti becomes the mission of the twelfth level, twelve strand DNA Avatar Jesheua-12/Tutankhamen/Joshua (Arcturian). Avatar 12/Tutankhamen/Joshua is none other than the child of Semenkhkare/Sabatoth and Nefertiti/Kiya/Ankhi, King Tutankhamen of Egypt.
- Jesheua-12/Tutankhamen is born to Semenkhkare/Sabatoth (Blue Flame Melchizedek) and Nefertiti/Kiya/Ankhi who hold the fifth degree code of advanced genetic burdens for ascension. From c. 1367-1352 BC, the Keepers of the Blue Flame led by qualified Serres-Egyptian-Melchizedeks at Giza, successfully ascend several thousand individuals not of Anu (Annanuki and Sirian hybrid Human) through the Halls of Amenti.

There is conflict between Serres-Egyptian-Melchizedeks and Anu-Melchizedeks

As a result of the conflict, Akhenaten/Moses accidently opens the portals to the underworld. The Halls of Amenti and the guardianship of the Ark of the Covenant is transferred to the Hibiru Cloister (Hebrew). The Blue Flame Melchizedek Essenes and Melchizedek Hibiru Cloisters are appointed by the Azurites of Ra to share guardianship over the Ark of the Covenant. The Melchizedeks are free from the DNA Seals of Amenti (seventh Seal, 7-D Seal). The Melchizedeks establish the Essene brotherhood (Keepers of the Blue Flame) and the priesthood of Melchizedeks. From this point forward, Nefertiti/Kiya/Ankhi will be referred to as Nefertiti.

At age nine, Jesheua-12/Tutankhamen is taken to Giza and trained by the Priests of UR for the ascension rights that he will be conducting for both Amunist (Anu-Melchizedek) and Atenist (Serres-Egyptian Melchizedek) believers.

The Ark of the Covenant

Complete Ark with pillar attached.

The image above depicts the complete Ark with its pillar attached. The device stood between 45 to 180 feet tall. The dimension of the Ark given in the book of Exodus represented a miniature version of the Egyptian original.

Jeshua-9/Jesus is born into the Essene community at Qumran. The Ark of the Covenant is kept at the Essene community in secret. At age 20 (8 AD) after studying in Persia and India, he is taken to Giza by the priests of Ur. Here Jeshua-9/Jesus assists many groups to ascend through the Halls of Amenti.[35]

The Ark of the Covenant, Sphere of Amenti, and the tools of the Rod and the Staff become closely guarded secrets, held within the confines of select Serres-Egyptian and Melchizedek Cloister families with whom the Priests of Ur maintain secret contact.

The image below is a drawing showing the complete Ark pillar superimposed onto the Human body.

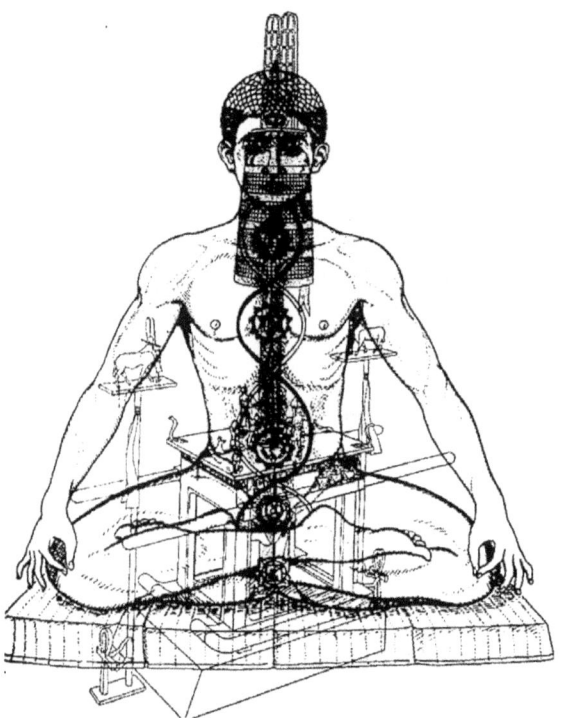

The complete Ark - Pillar superimposed on the human body, or the human bodhl, or enlightenment tree.

The Ark of the Covenant
Alien Device or Divine Artifact?

Akashic Record Reading (Robin White Turtle Lysne 7/18/19): *You (Stacy/Shakinah) were in the heart of darkness right from being a starseed. You incarnated into many lifetimes very quickly. Male and then female, female and then male.*

According to Parkes (2019), the teachings of RA seem to corroborate the notion that even the darkest energy eventually finds its way back to the light. Some souls take the darker route, opting for fire purification in order to explore the special difficulties and experiences of being a dark being. Parkes explains:

When we begin incarnation cycles, we begin as our darkest aspect on whatever "level" we are on. I can, as a light being, come into a frequency that is "dark" or slower and still easily reach the highest octave of that vibration and transcend it. If I came in as a low frequency dark being on that same vibration, I would easily be able to resonate with the lowest octave of the same vibration. But there is always free will. No one ever has to choose dark roles; it depends on your unique reason for being here. Judgment or feelings of victimization are part of playing the darker roles. Dark and light provide a perfect balance to this polarity planet of opposite polarities.

Incarnations

Incarnations happen again and again as a result of failure to *pass* Earth school. We die physically, and our eternal, atomic cluster of consciousness is brought back through rebirth into the same grade in order to pass on to the next higher grade. Progressing through our mobile highway of light energy, we encounter the experience of meeting other atoms of different elements of matter. With each new experience is added another atom of consciousness. Our consciousness increases in size, composed of many atoms of different experiences and of different elements. Our consciousness is composed of the same number of atoms as the number of experiences we have had since our creation as an individual. Experience is recorded in our consciousness. The consciousness is the eternal record of our knowing.[36]

Incarnation Back into Egypt

The Sirians, attempting to bring unity consciousness (divine feminine energy) into Egypt, interbreed with members of the Atlantean and Lemurian races creating a Human race known as the Serres-Egyptian Melchizedeks. During this time, Egypt was out of balance with an overabundance of masculine energy carried over from the Atlantean civilization, which was dominated by masculine energies. Winter (2019) suggests:

Circa 9500 years ago, the Templar-Anu regains control of Atlantis, while the Sirian-Council-Annanuki, the Anu-Melchizedeks, and Serres-Egyptians rebuild Egypt. Under the Templar-Anu rule, women are subservient and are used as breeding.

The Serres-Egyptians (Arcturian/Sirians) and the Lemurians of Earth interbreed, forming a new guardian race known as the Melchizedek Cloister. They are born with the Shield of the Arc in their genetic code and bear the Shield of the Arc (8% of the living population). Those bearing the Shield of the Arc become the Earth guardians of the Ark of the Covenant and the Sphere of Amenti. Winter (2019) suggests:

The Serres-Egyptians begin a new line of Egyptians bearing an advanced genetic strain, who later become the Melchizedek Cloister (new hybrid race evolved from the Nephilim) and orchestrate the Atenist movement redirecting the Egyptian culture back to the Law of One teachings of Akhenaten/Moses (Serres-Egyptian and Anu-Melchizedek), the great-grandson of Jacob/Israel.

The Melchizedek Cloister serve as a Host Matrix Family for the Anu (Annanuki and Sirian hybrid Human-Nephilim) and the Aton-A Host Matrix Family. This allows the Annanuki to advance the spiritual aspects of their evolution through working with the Law of One. For those of the Annanuki Resistance, the children of the Anu (Anu-Melchizedek/Israelites) become a target for infiltration by the Annanuki Resistance, those intent on destroying the Sphere of Amenti.[37]

Anu (Annanuki and Sirian hybrid Human-Nephilim) Are Worshiped as Gods

This is the time when the masses of Humanity perceive the Anu-Melchizedeks (Nephilim) as gods. The Egyptian dynasties are formed during the next eight thousand years and the Sumerian culture begins to flourish. During this time Thoth/Hermes as the reincarnation Enki/Enoch grant Humanity the use of *free will*.[38]

The Sirians create the great pyramid of Giza, which is built by Enki/Enoch (serpent—dragon), a descendant of the Sirians. Giza is considered the greatest power plant ever built on Earth. At the time of its use, it could furnish unfathomable amounts of power without a comparison in today's power production standards. The power of the pyramid of Giza comes from the ability to focus cosmic energy by mirroring three-dimensional reality. The ability to focus cosmic energy comes from the name pyramid. *Pyra* comes from the word *pyro*, which means fire, and *mid* means middle; fire in the middle refers to the focus of cosmic energy.[39]

- Thoth/Hermes (reincarnation of Enki/Enoch) is given ruling power and becomes (Jehovian-Anu).
- The Jehovian-Anu (Elohim Sirius A-Zeta) run the Galactic Federation and are in competition with the Templar-Anu (Annanuki hybrid program) agenda.
- Abram/Abraham is a Hibiru/Hebrew-Melchizedek and is the father of Jacob/Israel (Jehovian-Anu). The Israelites are formed when the Hibiru/Hebrew Melchizedeks and the Templar-Anu interbreed.
- Tuthmosis III/(King David) is Hibiru/Hebrew-Melchizedek and Templar-Anu.

The Hibiru/Hebrew were early metal-workers and chemists. Gold was bonded between magic, scientific knowledge, and religion during early civilizations on Earth.[40]

Mixing of the Races Begins

Tuthmosis III (King David) is the son of Osiris (Orion-Jehovian) and Isis (Serres- Egyptian-Hibiru/Hebrew). Tuthmosis III's (Nephilim) lineage begins the mixing of the Hibiru/Hebrew and Jehovian Annanuki races. Tuthmosis III rules from the age of five until his death at fifty-six (54 years - 1479 BC to 1425 BC). Tuthmosis III has three Canaanite wives and a large harem. Tuthmosis III has a child with Sarai/Sarah (Hibiru/Hebrew Melchizedek) whose name is Isaac. The image below is a statue of Tuthmosis III/King David.

Serres-Egyptian Royalty

Tuthmosis III/King David – Nephilim

Isaac begins the second Israelite lineage of the Hibiru/Hebrew, Jehovian Annanuki, and Templar-Anu, who become the Israelites.

The genograms below show the Royal and Biblical Lineages starting with the Israelites and the Royal House of Egypt, which includes the Royal Marriages, the lineages from Abram/

Abraham (Hibiru/Hebrew-Melchizedek), to twelfth level Avatar Jesheua-12 (Tutankhamen), and to Jeshua-9/Jesus (Essene).

Royal and Biblical Lineages

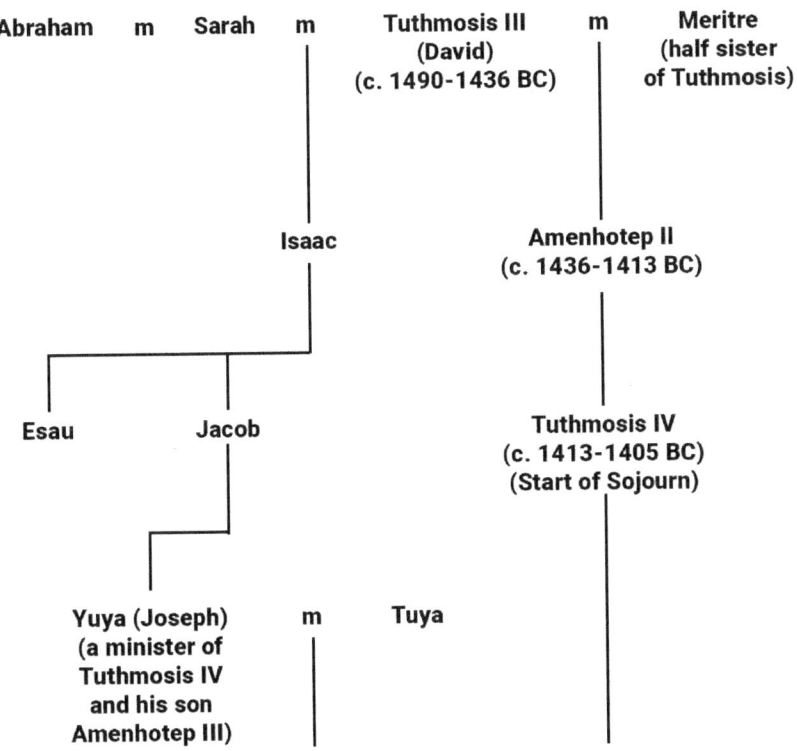

Original image modified by S. Ray, 2020.

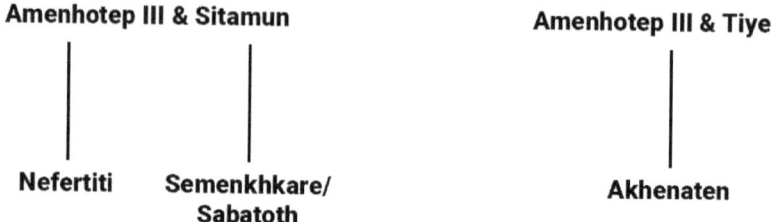

Amenhotep III & Sitamun (Annu-Melchizedek) parents of Nefertiti

Amenhotep III & Sitamun parents of Semenkhkare/Sabatoth

Amenhotep III & Tiye (Annu-Melchizedek) parents of Akhenaten (Annu-Melchizedek)

Timeline created by S. Ray, 2020.

Royal Marriages

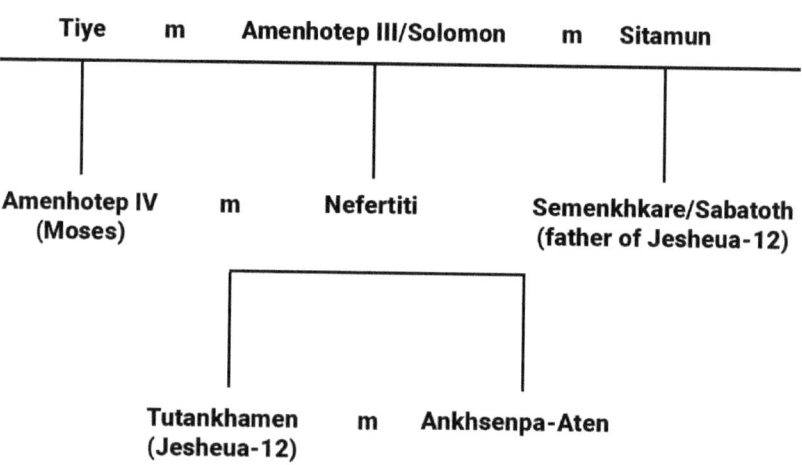

Timeline created by S. Ray, 2020.

Lineage from Abraham to Jesus

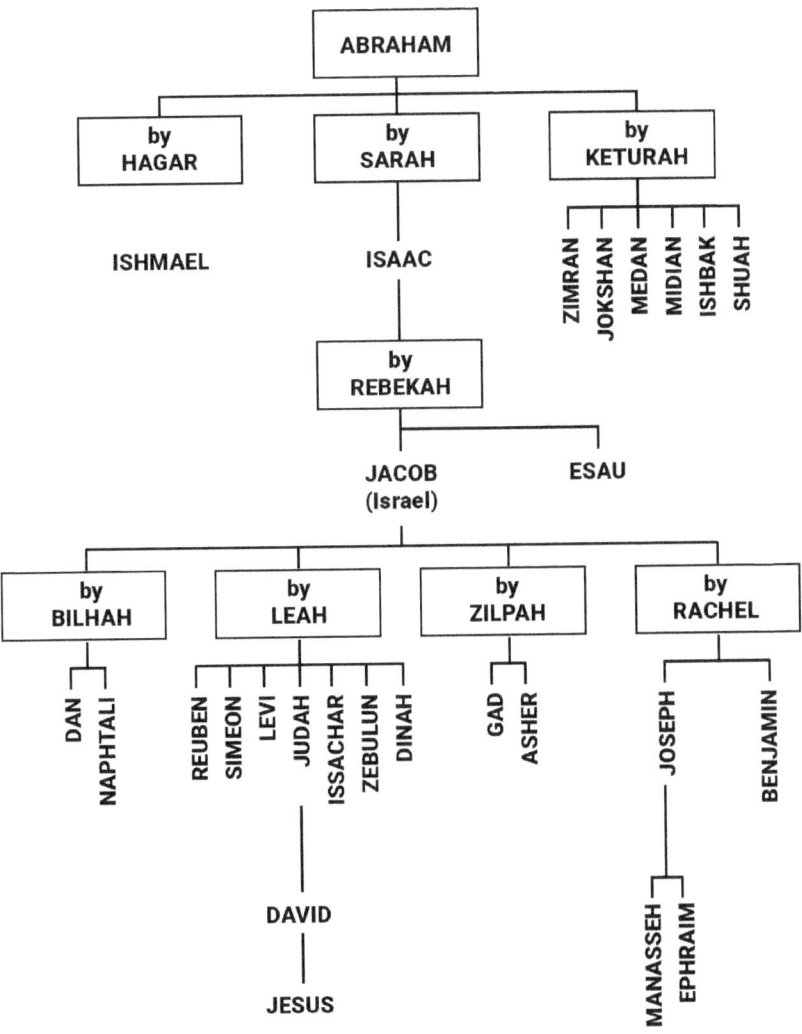

Original image modified by S. Ray, 2020.

Thoth/Hermes (Jehovian-Anu) brings ancient Atlantean knowledge into Egypt before the Pharaonic Dynasties form. Thoth is the keeper of knowledge passed down into the Halls of Amenti.[41]

The Serres-Egyptian Melchizedeks (fifth root race) are free from the DNA Seals of the Arc of Amenti, aka The Seal of Amenti (7-D Seal). They establish the Essene brotherhood and priesthood of Melchizedeks. Hopefully, through the Serres-Egyptian Melchizedeks, the Sphere of Amenti may be entered back into Earth's core following the Atlantean cataclysm.

Abram/Abraham (Hibiru/Hebrew-Melchizedek) and Sarai/Sarah (Hibiru/Hebrew-Melchizedek) Take a Trip from Ur into Egypt.

Priests of Ur are guardians of the Ark of the Covenant along with select Serres-Egyptians and Melchizedek Cloister families (Hibiru/Hebrews). Ur is located two hundred miles southeast of present-day Baghdad north of Canaan. The map below shows the Egyptian domain and Canaan during the time of Abram/Abraham.

Map of the Egyptian domain and Canaan during the time of Abram/Abraham.

It is my belief that Enki/Enoch (Jehovian Annanuki) directed Abram/Abraham to *Go from your country to the land I will show you. I will make you into a great nation* (Genesis 12:1-2) in an attempt to intermix the Hebrew Semitic (Serres-Egyptian Melchizedek Cloister) people with the Anu Egyptian Royalty. This is an ascension mission. Enki's children are trapped in the third dimensional (3D) Earth Time Matrix following the Atlantis cataclysm. Enki/Enoch is attempting the ascension of his children the Anu-Melchizedeks.

Isis ~ Mother of Tuthmosis III

Egyptian Iconography of Isis.

According to the biblical narrative, Canaan is the place of origin for Abram/Abraham (Hibiru/Hebrew-Melchizedek) and his wife Sarai/Sarah (Hibiru/Hebrew-Melchizedek). For a brief while, Tuthmosis III, King David (c. 1490–1436 BC), weds Sarai. Following her departure from Egypt with her first husband, Abram/Abraham, Sarai returns to Canaan to give birth to her son, Isaac (as described in the Bible). The Iconography above shows an engraved representation of the ancient Egyptian goddess Isis, who was the mother of Tuthmosis III (King David), on the wall of the Philae temple in Egypt.

The biological father of Isaac is Tuthmosis III. The second Israelite lineage is established with Sarai/Sarah and Pharaoh Tuthmosis III's conception of their child Isaac. Enki/Enoch tells Sarai/Sarah that her descendants will enter back into Egypt and claim what is rightfully theirs—foretelling the ascension mission that Akhenaten/Moses (Serres-Egyptian and Anu-Melchizedek) will initiate a return to the teachings of the Law of One that were previously corrupted in Atlantis. Isaac's lineage is Hibiru/Hebrew-Melchizedek (Sarai/Sarah) and Templar-Anu (Tuthmosis III).

Isaac's lineage will be brought back into Egypt to claim what is rightfully the Israelites' through Joseph/Yuya (Coat of many colors). The first lineage of the Israelites traces back to Tuthmosis III, the son of Isis (Serres-Egyptian princess), and Osiris (Orion-Jehovian), who brought the Atlantean knowledge of the Law of One from Atlantis into Egypt.

Upon returning to Canaan, as the Bible story states, Abram/Abraham fails to kill Isaac on the alter on Moriah. When Sarai/Sarah dies, Abram/Abraham adopts Isaac. Sarai/Sarah's descendants are the Israelites (Anu-Melchizedeks) that return to Egypt after four generations following their patriarch Joseph/Yuya. The Lord tells Abram that four generations of Sarai/Sarah's descendants will be strangers in another country, and the fourth generation will return (see Appendix B). See image below of Egyptian gods in Philae's temple complex, Egypt.

Egyptian gods in Philae's temple complex, Egypt.

From this point forward, Akhenaten/Moses will be referred to as Akhenaten. The understanding is that Akhenaten and Moses are the same man. Jesheua-12/Tutankhamen/Joshua will be referred to as Jesheua-12/Tutankhamen. Jesheua-12, Tutankhamen, and Joshua are the same man.

Son of Isaac (Templar-Anu and Serres-Egyptian Hebrew Melchizedek Cloister Canaanite) and Rebekah (Serres-Egyptian Hebrew Melchizedek Cloister Canaanite) is Jacob/Israel. Jacob is given the title Yidra-El (El means Elohim).

Jacob and Amenhotep III/Solomon are the great grandsons of Tuthmosis III (King David). Jacob is the father of a son Joseph (Yuya), and a son King David (Tuthmosis III). Joseph has a son Aaron/Ephraim, Jesheua-12/Tutankhamen's uncle.[42]

According to the Bible:

Abram/Abraham (Hibiru/Hebrew-Canaanite) lives 175 years
Sarai/Sarah (Hibiru/Hebrew-Canaanite) lives 127 years
Isaac (Anu Melchizedek-Israelite) lives 180 years
Jacob/Israel (Anu Melchizedek-Israelite) lives 147 years
Joseph/Yuya (Anu Melchizedek-Israelite) lives 110 years

Ruling Egyptian Pharaohs:

Tuthmosis III (King David)	Rules 54 years
Amenhotep II	Rules 23 years
Tuthmosis IV	Rules 8 years
Amenhotep III	Rules 38 years
Akhenaten (alone)	Rules 6 years [43]

The image below is a red granite carving of Amenhotep III/Solomon, eighteenth dynasty, c. 1400 BC from Thebes (British Museum, London).

Egyptian Stele of Amenhotep III/Solomon.

The Two Branches of Israelites (Anu-Melchizedeks) Are United

Amenhotep III/Solomon (great grandson of Tuthmosis III) marries Tiye (Yuya/Joseph's daughter) and the two branches of Israelites (Anu-Melchizedeks) are united. See image below for a granite sculpture of Queen Tiye, wearing the double-feathered crown with the sun disc and Hathor's horns, eighteenth dynasty, reign of Amenhotep III, c. 1391-1353 BC.

Granite Egyptian stele of Queen Tiye.

Chapter 3

ARMANA ~ ATENIST MOVEMENT

The Worship of the Sun God Aten

Turning Point ~ The link is restored between the Israelites (Anu-Melchizedek) and the Egyptian Royalty ~Anu ~ (Annanuki and Sirian hybrid Human) since Tuthmosis III (David from the Bible ~ ruling Egypt for 54 years) fathered Isaac (son of Sarai/Sarah and Abram/Abraham).

Anu (Annanuki and Sirian hybrid Human) and Serres-Egyptian (Hibiru/Hebrew Melchizedek Cloister) Are Intermixed

Interbreeding with the Melchizedek's Cloister and Sirian-Annanuki create the Nephilim, an Anu Human race. The Serres-Egyptians, *Anu-Melchizedeks,* and Hibiru/Hebrew people are now guardians of the Ark of the Covenant, retaining custody of the rod and staff of the Sphere of Amenti.

Sculpture by D. Chester, 1920.

The image above is a sculpture by Daniel Chester French (USA, c 1920), named *The Sons of God Saw the Daughters of Men That They Were Fair*. Genesis 6:4, *In those days as well as later, when the sons of the gods had intercourse with the daughters of mortals and children were born to them, the Nephilim were on the earth; they were the heroes of old, people of renown.*

The Aten cult shows up in Egypt at the time of
Tuthmosis IV (1413 -1405).
Worship of "Aten"
Tuthmosis IV appoints Yuya/Joseph (Anu-Melchizedek-Israelite)
as his minister.

The Sirians bring knowledge of Christ Consciousness to third dimensional (3D) Earth teaching the embodiment of the *golden light of the sun.* Christ consciousness means the Law of One. It refers to the understanding and awareness of our purpose as spiritual beings. The gold frequency is divine light and carries the energy of divine love and compassion. Sirius has been known as the *Blue Sun* and carries *Blue Frequency.* The deep blue light carries the codes of an advanced race of light beings who are in service of the divine plan and the evolution of the Milky Way Galaxy and Earth.

The Sirian Avatars Couples of Christ Consciousness

- Isis (Serres-Egyptian priestess) and Osiris (Orion-Jehovian)
- Akhenaten (Serres-Egyptian and Anu-Melchizedek) and Nefertiti (Serres-Egyptian-Melchizedek)
- Jesheua-12/Tutankhamen (Arcturian, Lyran, Sirian) and Ankhesenamun (Serres-Egyptian-Melchizedek)
- Jeshua-9/Jesus (Arcturian) and Mary Magdalene/Sophia (Arcturian, Sirian, and Lyran)

Together these couples embodied the Divine Masculine and Feminine frequencies of the Gold Frequency of Christ Consciousness and God/Elohim.

Israel is the illegitimate son of Egypt, who challenges his father to accept him.[44]

The image blow is a relief representing Akhenaten, worshiping the Aten sun disk. He ruled Egypt for about 17 years. He changed the state cult of Amun Ra to that of Aten and moved the capital from Thebes to Tell el-Amarna.

Iconography depicts Akhenaten worshipping the god Aten.

The Sea People Migrate to Egypt (1177 BC)

The sea people are known as the Phoenicians or *Khalu*. The Phoenicians (Khalu) are a Semitic-speaking people who migrate from the region of Cannon (Israel and Syria) into Egypt and are known as *Sheppard Kings*. The Phoenicians or *Canaanites* flourished between the first and second millennia BC living near the Atlantic and Mediterranean coasts and are believed to be Atlantean descendants.[45] Recent DNA testing shows that Phoenicians have European ancestry. The image below is a Phoenician mask (female protone) made from clay (sixth century BC, Carthage).

Phoenician mask (sixth century BC).

The Carthaginians were Phoenician colonists who came from the Near East's Mediterranean coast. They followed the Punic religion, a regional variant of the old Canaanite religion, and spoke the Semitic language of Canaanite. The Carthaginians established multiple colonies and traveled great distances across the oceans.

Tunis, the capital of Tunisia, has a beachfront district called Carthage, which is well-known for its historic archeological ruins. It was originally the capital of the great Carthaginian (Punic) Empire, which was overthrown by Rome in the second century BC. The Phoenicians founded it in the first millennium BC. It still has a dispersed assortment of historic theaters, baths, palaces, and other remains, many of which have expansive views of the Gulf of Tunis.

The Phoenicians evolved from the Canaanites, a Semitic tribe of the Middle East, which also gave birth to the people of Ugariti, the Hebrews (Jews) and later the Arabs. The Canaanites were the earliest inhabitants of Lebanon according to written historical records. They were called Sidonians in the Bible. Sidon was one of their cities. Artifacts unearthed at Byblos have been dated to 5000 BC. They were produced by Stone Age farmers and fishermen. They were repelled by Semitic tribes who arrived as early as 3200 BC.

Canaanites ousted the Hittites, invaders from present-day Turkey and overpowered the Ugarit people on the Syrian coast and drove southward until they stopped Ramases III, the pharaoh of Egypt. The Canaanites also had encounters with the Hyksos, a people who conquered lower kingdom of Egypt, and the Assyrians.

According to the Bible, the ancient Canaanites were idol worshipers who practiced Human sacrifice and engaged in deviant sexual activity. They reportedly conducted Human sacrifices in which children were immolated in front of their parents on stone altars, known as Tophets, dedicated to the mysterious dark god Molech. We have some idea of what the Canaanites looked like. An Egyptian iconograph from 1900 BC depicts Canaanite dignitaries visiting the pharaoh. The Canaanites have Semitic facial features and dark hair, which the women wear in long tresses, and the men have mushroom-shaped bundles on the tops of their heads. Both sexes wore bright red and yellow clothes, long dresses for women and kilts for the men. From what scholars have been able to ascertain, the Canaanites were a largely urban people that originated in eastern Syria, migrated southward along the Mediterranean, and lived mostly between the Jordan River and the Mediterranean Sea in what is now Israel. The ancient Canaanites were not a well-established empire and in fact were often overrun by the great empires of Mesopotamia, Egypt, and Anatolia. By c. 1100 BC, the ancient Canaanites virtually disappeared, blending into the Israelite lineages.

Egyptians and Israelites of Egypt

The early Egyptians made an agreement to serve and worship the Anu (Annanuki and Sirian hybrid Human-Nephilim) who created the Egyptian and Hebrew peoples through genetic manipulation. Egyptians and Israelites of Egypt are being used as slaves. Akhenaten, son of Tiye who is daughter of Yuya/Joseph, who is the grandson of Isaac—son of Saria/Sarah (Serres-Egyptian-Hibiru/Hebrew, holder of the fifth degree code) and Nefertiti are trying to help both Egyptians and Israelites to break free of the Annanuki resistance (Templar-Anu)[46].

Nefertiti a Sirian Starseed

Nefertiti is Serres-Egyptian-Melchizedek. She is the great granddaughter of Tuthmosis III (King David of the Bible), confirming her Israelite lineage. Her name, *Nefertiti,* means *the beautiful one.*[47] Nefertiti has a soothing voice that she uses during the temple ceremonies at Armana. She lives with her husband, Akhenaten, their four daughters, Tutankhamen, Semenkhkare/Sabatoth, Aye/Ephraim, and other Aten worshipers at Armana during the eighteenth dynastic period in Egypt.

The statue depicted here is from the eighteenth dynasty (c. 1351-1334) of the New Kingdom, Egypt's Tell el-Amarna. The image below shows Queen Nefertiti with an enlarged cranium, a characteristic common to the Melchizedek, Egyptian, and Serres lineages. The statue, which dates to the 18th dynasty, 1351-1334 BC, is situated near Tell el-Amarna, Egypt.

Statue of Queen Nefertiti, Tell el-Amarna, Egypt
(eighteenth dynasty 1351-1334 BC).

Nefertiti is brought to Earth as part of a larger plan of the seeding of Earth. The Sirians have already been active during the seeding and the settlements of Lemuria and Atlantis. They have influence during the Egyptian, Mayan, and African civilizations by providing advanced astronomical and medical information. The Sirians help build the pyramids in Egypt, Mayan civilization, Bosnia, and Australia. Moreover, they guide the construction of temples along with the many tunnels and pathways into inner Earth. In the future, they will be involved in establishing the new Golden Age of Aquarius on Earth in 2070 as we ascend back to 5D Terra. Nefertiti is a Sirian starseed.

Nefertiti's mission is to bring more love, light, and consciousness to the Egyptian culture by speaking from her heart. She is to witness, observe, and bring compassionate understanding and information from a higher source (divine messenger). Nefertiti attempts to bridge the Egyptian people and their consciousness to the higher realms (ascension). The image below is a standing striding figure of Nefertiti made of limestone. Originally from Amarna.

Figure of Nefertiti made of limestone.

The Sirians remind us of all that our bodies are from the Earth, but our Souls are from the Stars. As Master teachers, the Sirians bring information to Ancient Egyptians in order to help them remember who they are and where they are going. The Sirian starseeds teach the Egyptians the principles of ascension, which have been recorded on Egyptian pyramid and temple walls.

Akhenaten and Nefertiti/Kiya/Ankhi

Nefertiti and Akhenaten take an active role in establishing the Aten cult, a religious mythology that defined Aten, the sun, as the most important god and the only one worthy of worship during the Egyptian polytheistic religious period. Akhenaten and Nefertiti rule Egypt during the wealthiest periods of Ancient Egyptian history. Some scholars believe that Nefertiti rules briefly as Neferneferuaten after her husband's exile into Sinai, upper Egypt. In several Reliefs, Nefertiti is shown wearing the crown of a pharaoh or smiting her enemies in battle.[48]

Shrine stele showing Akhenaten, Nefertiti, and three daughters beneath the Aten exhibited in Neues Museum in Berlin.

Previous to Akhenaten and Nefertiti's rule of Egypt, the worship of the sun god, Aten, is part of the traditional Egyptian religion as well the worship of many other gods and goddesses. During the ninth year of their reign, Akhenaten makes the worship of Aten, a rayed solar disc, the official religion of Egypt. Replacing polytheistic worship of idols, including the worship of the god Amun with the worship the sun god, Aten, and hailing Aten as the absolute and universal Lord of all things is not entirely accepted by the Amunist (polytheistic, Anu-Melchizedek) priesthood of Egypt, who have spent their lives devoted to polytheistic worship, specifically Kemetic worship. Kemetic followers worship a few gods (Maat, Bastet, Anubis, Sekhmet, or Thoth, among others) but recognize the existence of every god. This worship generally takes the form of prayer, offerings, and setting up altars. The stele below shows Akhenaten depicted as a sphinx at Armana with solar rays bathing him.

Akhenaten as a sphinx at Armana.

Akhenaten makes himself and Nefertiti the only representatives of the god Aten. Akhenaten's reign of Egypt lasts for 17 years, which ends around 1336 BC.[49] The carved stone, stele below depicts Nefertiti worshipping the Aten. She is given the title of Mistress of the Two Lands. On display at the Ashmolean Museum, Oxford.

Egyptian stele of Nefertiti worshipping the Aten.

The pioneering spiritual experiment led by Akhenaten and Nefertiti was intended to help the collective revere and experience a higher light. However, it was a failure only in that it was short-lived. It did manage to plant a new and quite powerful seed of light in the collective consciousness. This seed of light became a reference point for the coming three monotheistic religions of Judaism, Christianity, and Islam. Unfortunately, this seed of light picked up much negative programming from the 3D Matrix that needs to be cleared. Programming such as the God Force being viewed as exclusively masculine, the impulse to block other forms of worship, and elitism where only the chosen few could communicate with the God Force. Akhenaten and his wife Nefertiti could directly connect with the Aten. Akhenaten and Nefertiti were in effect the High Priest and High Priestess of the New Religion and finally that of persecution, violence, and death (which is how the experiment ended). All of these programs affected the coming three monotheistic religions in various degrees.[50]

Royal Egyptian and Israelite Lineage

Amenhotep III marries his infant sister Sitamun in order to inherit the Egyptian Royal throne. Amenhotep III then marries Tiye (Yuya/Joseph's daughter). In addition, Amenhotep III has seven foreign wives. Amenhotep is an original Aten worshiper, which included the worship of other deities. The image below is a statue of Tiye and Amenhotep III with one of their daughters.

Tiye, Amenhotep III, and one of their daughters.

Tiye and Amenhotep III

Amenhotep III (meaning Amun is Satisfied) was the ninth pharaoh of the eighteenth dynasty. According to different authors, he ruled Egypt from June 1386 BC to 1349 BC or June 1388 BC to December 1351 BC. Tiye and Amenhotep III had several surviving children. Her eldest daughter, Sitamun, was elevated to the position of Great Royal Wife by her father around the thirtieth year of his reign. She had her own apartments in the royal city of Malqata, across the hall from her father. She also may have intended to be buried in Amenhotep III's tomb, but it not clear if she was ever buried there. Another daughter, Isis or Iset, was also a Great Royal Wife of Amenhotep III. Two more daughters are known named Henuttaneb and Nebetah.

Tiye and Amenhotep III had at least two sons. Crown Prince Thutmose was a High Priest of Ptah before he predeceased his father. Their second son was originally known as Amenhotep IV. After his father's death and when he took the throne, he changed his name to Akhenaten and moved the capital city to a new site in Middle Egypt, which was also called Akhenaten. Tiye and Amenhotep III had another son named Semenkhkare, brother of Nefertiti, successor of Akhenaten (for a short period), the father of Jesheua-12/Tutankhamen.

Throughout his rule, Amenhotep III built various structures for his Queen Tiye. He devoted several of his shrines to her and also constructed a temple dedicated to her in Segeinga, Nubia. Here Tiye was worshipped as the goddess Hathor Tefnut, and she was also displayed as a sphinx. Tiye's temple was the female counterpart to the larger temple of Amenhotep III.

After Amenhotep III/Solomon and Tiye's wedding, Amenhotep III presents her with the frontier fortress of Zarw (in the area of modern Quantara East of the Suez Canal) as a kind of summer palace so that she could be near her Israelite relatives. The frontier of Zarw is located beyond Egypt proper because shepherds (Israelites) are still viewed by Egyptians as an *abomination*.[51]

Queen Tiye (eighteenth dynasty, Egypt).

Most importantly, Amenhotep III gifted Tiye a pleasure lake at the city of Djaruka, which her husband sent out another commemorative scarab detailing the lake. This lake may have been similar to the lake that was built at the royal city of Malqata. See image below for the Pleasure Lake Scarab.

Pleasure Lake Scarab, Amenhotep III and Tiye's Marriage Scarab.

Nefertiti, the Egyptian queen, and the Great Royal Wife (chief consort) of Akhenaten is Akhenaten's half-sister through their father Amenhotep III/Solomon. The name Solomon has origins in the Semitic language and refers to *salam* or Hebrew *shalom*, meaning *peace*.

Akhenaten's mother (Tiye) is a non-Amunite (part Israelite). Nefertiti, wife of Akhenaten, is the daughter of Amenhotep III/Solomon and Sitamun. Sitamun's parents are Tuthmosis IV and Mut Muya. Nefertiti's great-grandfather is Tuthmosis III (Templar-Anu) and her great-great grandmother is Isis (Serres-Egyptian). The image below is a sculpture of Tiye.

Egyptian Stele of Tiye.

Holleman (2016) suggests in his second book *Empires of Gold, Iron and God* that Yuya/Joseph is the Israelite Patriarch Joseph (from the Bible) and the Egyptian Grand Vizier. He is the son of Jacob and the grandson of Isaac from the Bible. Yuya/Joseph is a nonroyal, wealthy landowner and serves as an Egyptian courtier appointed by Amenhotep II.

Among Yuya/Joseph's children are a son Aye who is also Aaron/Ephraim (from the Bible) who rules for a four-year period after Tutankhamen's death. Yuya/Joseph's daughter is Tiye, Akhenaten's mother.

- Amenhotep III (Anu-Melchizedek) and Sitamun (Anu-Melchizedek) are Nefertiti's parents.
- Amenhotep III (Anu-Melchizedek) and Tiye (Anu-Melchizedek) are Akhenaten's parents.

Nefertiti is Akhenaten's half-sister through their father Amenhotep III. Akhenaten's mother is non-Amunite (part Israelite), which makes Akhenaten (great-grandson of Jacob) Israelite and Egyptian. This means that Akhenaten is of the tribe of Ephraim (who later become the Jewish people) and of the tribe of Levi.[52]

Tiye, Akhenaten's mother, has two brothers: Anen, a priest of Heliopolis, and Aye/Aaron/Ephraim, general of the chariots.[53]

Aye/Aaron/Ephraim.

Yuya/Joseph (the son of Jacob and the grandson of Isaac from the Bible) is Akhenaten's grandfather and serves as an Egyptian courtier during the eighteenth dynasty of Egypt (see Appendix C). He is married to Tuya, an Egyptian noblewoman involved in many religious cults and is a member of the royal family. Their daughter Tiye (Anu-Melchizedek and Israelite) becomes the wife of Amenhotep III and is the mother of Akhenaten/Amenhotep IV. The previous image is a painting of Aye/Aaron/Ephraim, Yuya/Joseph's son, by Francesco Hayez.

Tiye has a brother Aye/Aaron/Ephraim, a successor of Tutankhamun. Aye is the second son of Yuya/Joseph (the son of Jacob and the grandson of Isaac from the Bible). Aye is also Aaron/Ephraim from the Bible. Aye was known to be the power behind the throne of Tutankhamun's reign. Aye remains in Egypt during the first exodus during the eighteenth Dynastic period, while Akhenaten is exiled in Sinai. Aye is the protector of Jesheua-12/ Tutankhamen. During the second exodus (Nineteenth Dynastic period), Aye follows Akhenaten out of Egypt and serves as Akhenaten's protector (general of the Chariots) and is also one of the founders of the twelve tribes of Israel. Aye later inherits most of the titles that Tiye's father (Yuya/Joseph) held at the court of Amenhotep III/Solomon during his lifetime (Holleman, 2016). According to Sepehr (2016), Chariots were introduced to Egyptian kings via the Hyksos. The Hyksos, a people of mixed Semitic and Asian descent, invaded Egypt and settled in the Nile delta c. 1640 BC. They formed the fifteenth and sixteenth dynasties of Egypt and ruled a large part of the country until driven out c. 1532 BC. The stele below shows Aye/Aaron/Ephraim receiving the Gold of Honor award in his Amarna tomb from Akhenaten.

Aye/Aaron/Ephraim receiving the Gold of Honor.

Tutankhamun marries Ankhesenamun, his half-sister, daughter of Akhenaten and Nefertiti. Tutankhamun serves as coregent while his father is in exile for 28 years. Tutankhamun's reign starts when he is ten years old and lasts nine years. Tutankhamun spends the first four years of his leadership at Amarna with his mother, Nefertiti. Despite the fact that Tutankhamen allowed the temples of the gods and goddesses to be reopened in Egypt during his fourth year of leadership (Amunist worship, polytheistic, Anu-Melchizedek), Tutankhamun remains an Atenist retaining his father's Aten religion.[54]

Egyptian Royalty Priestess of Amun ~ Tuya (Thuya) ~

Tuya (aka, Thuya) was an Egyptian noblewoman, the mother of queen Tiye and the wife of Yuya/Joseph. She is the grandmother of Akhenaten and great-grandmother of Jesheua-12/Tutankhamen.

The image below is of a small mask of gilded plaster jar that held one of Tuya's internal organs.

A small mask of gilded plaster (right) capped a mummy-like bundle that held one of Tuyu's internal organs. Each bundled organ was deposited in a stone jar with a head-shaped stopper like this (left).

The image below is a statue of Priestess of Amun ~Tuya, wife of Joseph.

Yuya/Joseph, Son of Jacob and Grandson of Isaac ~
The image below is the mummy of Yuya/Joseph, great grandfather (not by biology) to Jesheua-12/Tutankhamen.

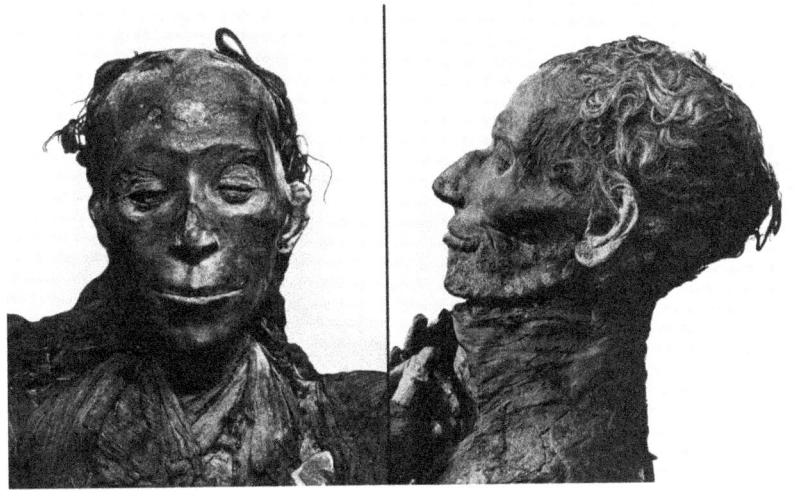

The mummy of King Tut's great grandfather, Yuya, is a stunning example of ancient Egyptian embalming. He and his wife were probably between 50 and 60 years old at the time of death. Like her husband, Tuyu was identified by inscriptions on funerary equipment. Hieroglyphs spell out her name and titles, which include dresser to the king, chantress of the god Amun, and lady of the harem of the god Min.

National Geographic (2019)

Yuya/Joseph marries Tuya (private nurse to Amenhotep III) and has a daughter, Tiye. Amenhotep III/Solomon grows up with Tiye and falls in love with her. As a result, Amenhotep III marries Tiye. Amenhotep III and Tiye have a son, Amenhotep IV/Akhenaten. Akhenaten's mother, Tiye (Anu-Melchizedek) is an Israelite, which makes Akhenaten Israelite and Egyptian Royalty. See image below of a statue of Amenhotep III.

Stone Stele of Amenhotep III.

Mother and Daughter

These images are statues of Tuya and her daughter, Tiye.

The image to the left is Tuya's gilded coffin. Tuya was the wife of Yuya/Joseph and mother of Tiye.

Gilded coffin of Tuya, Yuya/Joseph's wife.

Tiye ~Daughter of Yuya/Joseph and Tuya. Queen Tiye is wearing the double-feathered crown with the sun disc and Hathor's horns in the image above.

Human-2 Avatar ~ Akhenaten/Moses

Winter, 2019, further explains that in 1398 BC, Amenhotep IV (Akhenaten) Human-2 Avatar pure Annanuki Sirian council of 9D frequencies is born in Thebes, Egypt, to Anu-Melchizedek Mother Queen Tiye and Serres-Egyptian Father Amenhotep-III (Anu-Melchizedek). The Melchizedeks are free from the DNA seal of Amenti (7-D Seal). The Melchizedek Cloister holds the 5D gene code. The Melchizedeks establish the Essene brotherhood (descendants of Akhenaten) and priesthood of Melchizedeks. The Human lineage is of the Melchizedek cosmic family strain (a tonal signature). The Melchizedeks are a blended race carrying various racial strains. Though they represent the Cloister that originally began the yellow-skinned races on Earth, they are not limited to manifesting through this racial line. The Anu (Annanuki and Sirian hybrid Human-Nephilim) also hold the 5D key as they are seeded through the Melchizedek Cloister. Those who hold the 5D key gene code become the guardians of the Ark of the Covenant.

Amenhotep IV ~ Akhenaten/Moses ~ (Serres-Egyptian and Anu-Melchizedek/Israelite)

The interbreeding with the Melchizedek Cloister and Sirian-Annanuki create the Nephilim, an Anu Human race. Because of their advanced genetic package, the Melchizedeks are able to pass through the Blue Flame in the Halls of Amenti and experience teleportation through the portals into the Terran environment. The Melchizedeks established the Essene Brotherhood and Priesthood of Melchizedek, a priesthood that still exists on Earth today. The Cloister mix of Hibiru and Melchizedek became the Hebrew people (Christian lineages) and still carries a genetic advancement (burden for ascension). Two primary groups have evolved out of the original Melchizedek Cloister: the Cloistered family of Melchizedeks and the Templar- Melchizedeks (Templar-Anu). Templar-Melchizedeks (Templar-Anu) will have a distinctly patriarchal slant, often promoting gender subservience, elitist philosophy, and subjugation of Earth's elemental kingdom.

The Templar-Melchizedeks (Templar-Anu) are not originally part of the Cloister Family Melchizedeks but are a product of ET distortion and have created tensions and greatly influenced the development of many of our world religions.

The egalitarian Melchizedeks became known as the Speakers of the Blue Flame about 10,000 years ago (c. 8000 BC) when the Priesthood of Ur and the Palaidorian Council of Terra transferred Earth guardianship of the Staff of Amenti/ Blue Flame/Terra's morphogenetic field out of the hands of the unbalanced, patriarchal Melchizedek Priesthood and into the hands of the balanced Melchizedek Priesthood. The Cloister Melchizedek Priests of Ur disassociated themselves from the patriarchal Melchizedeks, attributing their elitist, sexist slant to infiltration of the Sirian-Annanuki cultures, who brought with them to Atlania, and later Atlantis, the distorted teachings of the original Templar Solar Initiates whose elitist, aggressive misuse of power for materialistic gain had culminated in the cataclysm of Terra c. 550,000,000 years ago. This transfer of guardianship of the power of the Blue Flame 10,000 years ago resulted in the instrumentation of two more genetic frequency seals being placed upon members of the sixth race Melchizedek Cloisters, who are associated with Templar distortions of the Sacred Law of One, and also on any descendants of the Templar-Melchizedeks or races who interbred with them and picked up their genetic coding.[55]

The Templar Seal is administrated about 3,500 years ago when descendants of Templar-Sealed Melchizedeks infiltrated Egyptian culture and violated the Covenant of Palaidor by opening the D-2 Earth portals as a way of orchestrating ascension through the D-1 and D-2 underworld. Through their misdeeds, many chaotic forces are unleashed upon the Earth, and Humans with distorted morphogenetic imprints are released from the Seals of Palaidor and Amenti and allowed to pass into Terra. Many tragic events since took place on Terra as a result of this misadventure, and a 7-D Seal is added to the Templar-Melchizedeks, who participated in these events. The Elohim now allows Humans who gain their favor through serving the truth of the sacred Law of One to pass through the Templar-Axion Seal. This distortion is passed on genetically as the Melchizedeks and their Hebrew hybrids interbreed with other racial strains.[56]

The Templar Seals still affect a majority of the present Human population. The Arcturians, Elohim, Pleiadeans, Sirian Council, and other assistants from the higher Harmonic Universes are still working to assist unintended Templar Seal bearers. Through spiritual training, Humans are led to at least a rudimentary understanding of the sacred Law of One. If the Seals are unwarranted, the Elohim petition the Ra Confederacy to remove any trace of the Templar Seals.[57]

The Melchizedek Order

The Melchizedek Order was believed to be the keepers of the occult knowledge. Melchizedek Order determined that destruction had to be stopped. Evolution and destruction are opposite polarities of the same energetic force. Evolution and destruction must occur at the same pace to keep the Universal energy in balance. If evolution is stopped, so is destruction. The *Fall of Man* was enacted by members of the Melchizedek Order to stop evolution, thereby stopping destruction until a solution could be found to heal the entire Universe. However, it is now known that the Melchizedek Order is a group of souls who are fractured and have been manipulating Humans.

The Spiritual Leadership of the Time

The spiritual leadership of the time realized that the initiations had to be stopped until a solution to the problem could be found. This solution has been found and corrected within the new genetic information extracted from Sirian form that, when embraced, now make it impossible for these beings to merge with the crystalline form here on Earth. These beings, who have also been unable to evolve and had been removed from their own natural environment, will be returned to their Universe as the interdimensional tear is repaired at the appropriate time within third dimensional evolution. They will also be released from our planet as Earth takes her ascension. Our fifth dimensional (5D) vibration will no longer be suitable for their presence.

To sever the Unconscious, the Melchizedek Order altered the orbit of another planet within our Solar System, known as Nibiru. Nibiru's orbit, which originally was just outside of the planet Pluto, was stretched to an orbit with an approximate 3,600-year cycle around the sun. Nibiru, in astrological terms, rules the Unconscious, and it is within Nibiru's Akashic Records that the records of the unconscious plane of reality are stored. As Nibiru pulled far enough away from our Solar System, the Unconscious ceased to have an influence over Humanity.[58]

If the Ra Confederacy agrees, the Seals are removed, and the incarnates' consciousness is allowed to pass through the eighth dimension where the DNA imprint in the morphogenetic field is repaired. Others who rightfully bear the Templar Seals may find freedom through working with the lessons of love, unity, and equality as taught through the sacred Law of One. When these lessons are learned, the incarnates' consciousness is no longer a threat to interplanetary security, and assistance in lifting the Templar Seals is provided. The Templar Seals create a separation within the astral awareness, creating a *lower* and *higher* astral identity.

The lower astral identity becomes known as the *evil twin* or the *dweller on the threshold* within some religious teachings. The Second Strand Distortion creates a division within the 2D elemental/emotional body, which creates two levels of the subconscious mind: a higher level of mind and lower level. The higher level holds identity fragments of subpersonalities, while the lower level creates a chaotic emotional force that comes to be known as *the shadow self,* exaggerating the Human's primitive emotional impulses.

The Axion Seal requires that the soul continue innumerable cycles of birth and rebirth until the time when Terra and Earth will merge. The sixth base tone of the first strand, sixth base tone of the fifth strand, and sixth base tone of the sixth strand of DNA are all removed from the morphogenetic field with the Templar-Axion Seal. The genetic configuration of the Templar-Axion Seal is the original meaning behind the symbolism of the 666, and these numbers also figured prominently in the earlier building of the Great Pyramid of Giza. This Seal originally applied to the Sirian-Annanuki who assisted in the construction of Giza. The 666 trademark becomes attached to the members of the Sirian-Annanuki who refused to abide by and uphold the Law of One. The 666 becomes part of the Human genetic code through the interbreeding of the Melchizedek Cloister with visiting Annanuki, who create the hybrid Anu races, the Nephilim (Annanuki and Sirian hybrid Human, see chapter 2, The Seal of Amenti or the 7-D Seal).

To administer the Templar-Axion Seal, part of the morphogenetic field is put under the jurisdiction of the Arcturian races. The soul's essence will have to evolve a disembodied consciousness, first through the Pleiadean system, then Arcturus, and then into Andromeda, before it can finally rebirth on Terra. Once the Terran cycle is complete, the soul returns to Earth. By passing one's consciousness through these other star systems, teachings of the Law of One slowly heals the individual's soul imprint, and there is no longer a need to return to 3D Earth. Ascension into Terra is possible, and the Covenant of Palaidor is fulfilled.

Due to the Templar and Templar-Axion Seals, the concept of *soul harvesting* becomes part of many religious teachings. The soul harvesting concept refers to souls bearing the Templar Seals being brought by one of the helper organizations before the Ra Confederacy for review, at which time those souls are deemed safe for transit to Terra or higher systems. At this point, the soul is released from the Templar Seals and allowed to end the perpetual cycles of birth and rebirth on Earth.

Those passing the review will have evolved to comprehension of the necessity for the Law of One and will have actively employed these principles within their present incarnation. Passing the review means the soul is *harvested* or cleared of its distortions and allowed to ascend to Terra for rebirth within the sixth and seventh races, and following its completed Terran cycles, the soul ascends out of matter. In some traditions, this concept became translated as *judgment day* or similar ideas of having to *passed God's test* and become *worthy*. But in truth, God's Universe is free, and these concepts applied only to beings bearing the Templar Seals, who wore the armor of their disregard for the Law of One within the configurations of their genetic codes. Processes of initiation that developed through the mystery schools of old and those of the present were all designed to assist in the ascension passage. Many are designed specifically to release the Templar Seals and to protect individuals from inadvertently adopting the Seals through interbreeding.

Many people of present-day Earth carry some portion, or all, of the Templar Seals, and they will experience such a review after passing into the astral plane in death. Others may begin this review before death by working with spiritual principles and guardians/ascended masters, who will help them learn the Law of One. In this way, the Seals are removed prior to death, which will allow some individuals to transmute the body and pass through the Halls of Amenti to Terra, immortalizing the body as it was originally intended. The enforced tour of duty of some of the Templar Seal bearers is almost at its end, as the merger of Earth's grid and Terra will take place within the next three to four Earth generations, a process that began in the year 2012. The seals are now lifting as we collectively raise our consciousness, breaking free of the 3D by following the original teachings of the Law of One.

Earth Inhabitants and Lineage History

- Cloister mix of Hibiru + Melchizedek = Hebrews
- Melchizedeks Cloister + Sirian-Annanuki = Nephilim
- Hibiru/Hebrew-Melchizedek + Templar-Anu = Israelites

Melchizedek Cloisters Hold the 5D Gene Code and Establish the Essenes

The image below shows an Essene staircase leading to an Essene compound located above the shores of the Dead Sea—one of the caves where the Dead Sea Scrolls were discovered by a passing shepherd.

Essene Compound.

Chapter 4

ANCIENT EGYPTIAN RELIGION

Osman (2019).

Ahmed Osman, an ancient Egyptian religion author, contends that Christianity has its roots not from Judaea but from Egypt. Through his research, Osman traces Egyptian history and compares Biblical figures such as Moses (Akhenaten), Phinehas (Pa-Nehesy), Joseph (Yuya) as counterparts and one and the same. When the Alexandria library is burned, evidence to support Osman's theories are lost.

Osman (2005) supports the idea that Christianity is a version of the ancient Egyptian cult of Serapis. In the Serapis belief, the holy family is made up of Osiris (Orion-Jehovian), the Egyptian god of the underworld, and Isis, Serres-Egyptian Priestess (Melchizedek Cloister) and their son Horus (hawk-headed Tuthmosis III/King David). This story tells how King Osiris was murdered by his jealous brother Set (the shadow energy). As a result, Osiris descended into the underworld where he was found by his wife, Isis (Sirian), who used her magic to conceive a son, Horus, who became the New Warrior King, Tuthmosis III/King David. The story of Isis and Osiris is brought to the Collective Consciousness by the Sirians. In this way, the Sirian teachers ensured that as we move forward in evolution, Humanity would not forget that energy moves in cycles on Earth and endings and new beginnings are part of the *mechanisms* of timelines and time cycles of renewal and rebirthing (see Appendix D).

Lineages from Tuthmosis III/King David.

- Tuthmosis III/King David – Son of Amun-Anu (Sirian Annanuki and Melchizedek Cloister/Nephilim

- Amenhotep II – Anu-Melchizedek
- Tuthmosis IV – Anu-Melchizedek
- Amenhotep III – Anu-Melchizedek: Amenhotep III fathers Amenhotep IV/Akhenaten (Serres-Egyptian and Anu- Melchizedek) with Tiye (Anu-Melchizedek/Israelite)

Joseph/Aye (Anu-Melchizedek/Israelite) bridges the Nephilim (Serres-Egyptian/Lemurian, Isis's descendants) and Israelites (Sarai's descendants) when he has a daughter Tiye. Tiye gives birth to Amenhotep IV/Akhenaten, who changes Egypt forever.

The Egyptian dynasties between the fifteenth and fourteenth centuries BC (second Egypt) begin with figures such as Abram/Abraham (Hibiru/Hebrew Melchizedek) sharing his wife Sarai/Sarah (Hibiru/Hebrew Melchizedek) with Tuthmosis III/King David (Nephilim-Annanuki and Serres-Egyptian), which leads to the birth of Isaac (the second of the Israelite lineages). The second Israelite lineage is brought back into Egypt by Joseph/Aye (coat of many colors) leading to the birth of Akhenaten's (Serres-Egyptian and Anu-Melchizedek) and the worship of Aten.

The short reign of Jesheua-12/Tutankhamen (Lyran, Arcturian, and Sirian) is an attempt to bridge and bring peace to those worshiping polytheistic deities (Amunists) and those worshiping one god (Atenists). However, as Osman (2004) states so eloquently, *the world was not yet ready to see these visions* of unity and integration (p. 237). The Israelites, being opposed to worship of multiple deities and gods, simply transposed polytheistic deities into a Christian form with the same recognition of the Holy archangels.

Attempt to Bridge the Factions
Eagle (Atenist, Serres-Egyptian Melchizedek) and Serpent (Amunist, polytheistic, Anu-Melchizedek)

Jesheua-12/Tutankhamen's mission is to act as a bridge. The eagle and serpent may be equated with the masculine strength and control over the physical world, as opposed to the feminine path of spiritual growth/higher knowledge. Will our Human lineage be directed by military conquest and control (eagle) or by higher knowledge and balance (serpent)? The eagle represents Enlil's influence on Humanity, and the serpent represents Enki/Enoch's influence on Humanity. Most of the world's spiritual traditions speak of polarities and dualistic perception: upward and downward, sky and water, wisdom and love, yin and yang, Shiva and shakti. Through the divine union of masculine and feminine, a new consciousness arises. There is a collapse of duality, representing the union of all aspects of self, pure love, and the Law of One.

Recent molecular genetics and advanced CT scanning of Jesheua-12/Tutankhamen's mummy shows that he had a curved spine, and his left foot was clubbed, with some of the bones in his toes decaying from a degenerative disease. Jesheua-12/Tutankhamen's reign began more than 3,000 years ago when he was nine years old and lasted less than a decade.

The next image is a gold funerary mask of Jesheua-12/Tutankhamen displaying the eagle and the serpent.

Jesheua-12/Tutankhamen's gold funerary mask displaying the Eagle and the Serpent.

Akhenaten ~ Egyptian Royalty (Serres-Egyptian Anu-Melchizedek/Israelite)

The next images provide historical, archeological, and spiritual information about Akhenaten and Nefertiti.

Akhenaten

Akhenaten

➢ Pharaoh Akhenaten dreamed of a world where individuals lived in peace and harmony, were equal under the law, and served each other. Akhenaten was a man with a mission; of rare intelligence and deep perception, with great sensitivity and a gift for words, and possessing an intense desire for universal peace and understanding.

➢ Akhenaten's truth was that all things are One, all beings are One, and there is no right or wrong in the One. He symbolized the One as a golden disc projecting out invisible rays of love/ light terminating in life-giving ankhs. Just as the rays of the sun fructify the Earth, the rays of love/ light offer ever-lasting life for mankind.

Cosmic harmony was the model for earthly harmony in Akhenaten's temples. Intellectual life was part of the spiritual life; mental life was a reflection of the divine life; and Ascension was the most important ideal to strive for. This holistic philosophy accounted for the variety, complexity, and multiplicity of life, but never implied separation; unity was always present. To acquire knowledge was to observe the divine at work; all branches of learning were divine. Science was incorporated into the highest exaltation of knowledge:

Theosophical Society, Phillips (2017).

Nefertiti ~ Serres-Egyptian Royalty

Nefertiti

> As a vital part of Pharaoh Akhenaten's transformation of Egypt, Queen Nefertiti was the embodiment of the Sacred Wisdom of Isis which confirms that the sahu survives the physical death of the body. At the heart of the Sacred Wisdom of Isis is the practice of Opening of the Way which alters the khat or physical body, and its etheric twin, the ka or spiritual body, in order to release the sahu.

Nefertiti

> The Sacred Wisdom of Isis teaches that the ka or Soul is the more feminine aspect of the mind-body-spirit complex and that the ba or Ego represents the masculine. Soul urges and Ego does. Soul provides the dream and Ego the manifestation. Balancing Soul and Ego, then, is the goal of the Sacred Wisdom of Isis.

Theosophical Society, Phillips (2017).

Timeline for Akhenaten's Atenist Movement
Life ~ Universal Power
One with Nature and Others

- 1395 BC, Akhenaten (Amenhotep IV) is born to Amenhotep III/Solomon and Queen Tiye.
- 1384 BC, Semenkhkare/Sabatoth is born as a Blue Flame Holder, embodied by the Melchizedek Cloister Flame. He later becomes a High Priest of Akhenaten's Atenist movement.
- 1378 BC, Akhenaten (Amenhotep IV), age 16, is given the position of coregent with his father, Amenhotep III/Solomon.
- 1366 BC, The Halls of Amenti are opened after Earth's grid frequencies have stabilized. Akhenaten is taken by the priests of UR to inner Earth for the ascension training that he will be conducting. The Urites establish the Priesthood of UR and live primarily underground and within inner Earth. They serve as guardians of the Ark of the Covenant.
- 1367 BC, Amenhotep III/Solomon dies.
- 1367 BC, Akhenaten begins to rule Egypt alone. Akhenaten is 28.
- 1363 BC, Amenhotep IV changes his name to Akhenaten or Aton.
- 1362 BC, Akhenaten is instructed by priests of UR to relocate to Amarna, where inner Earth portals lay beneath and creates the city of Armana, where he will worship Aten and the Law of One. Through the portals

located beneath Armana, Akhenaten and his priestly order may reach the Ark of the Covenant through portal passages and the Halls of Amenti. The Serres-Egyptian lineage of priests who are anti-Atenist will try to stop this. Akhenaten successfully ascends his people for five years.

- 1361 BC, Jesheua-12/Tutankhamen at age ten is given the throne. His mission is to integrate the Amunist (polytheistic, Anu-Melchizedek) and Atenist (Serres-Egyptian Melchizedek) factions in order to bring peace to Egypt.
- 1357 BC, Jesheua-12/Tutankhamen changes his name to Tutankhamun in order to bridge a compromise between his Aten beliefs and those of the Amunist priests.
- 1357 BC, Akhenaten exiles to Sanai.
- 1352 BC, Semenkhkare/Sabatoth (Blue Flame Melchizedek) is executed for his participation in the ascension activities and for his knowledge of the Ark of the Covenant. Semenkhkare/Sabatoth has been imprisoned since 1361 BC.

The ancient Egyptians understood that their gods have prevailed over the forces of chaos through the creation of the world and relied upon Humanity's help to maintain it. The people of Mesopotamia hold this same belief but feel they are coworkers with the gods, laboring daily to hold back chaos through even the simplest acts. The Egyptians believe all they have to do is recognize how the world works and who is responsible for its operation and behave accordingly.

This behavior is directed by the central cultural value, *ma'at* (harmony and balance), which is sustained by an underlying force known as *heka* (magic). *Heka* (personified as the god Heka) has been present from the creation of the world, preexisting the gods, and allows those gods to perform their duties. All the people, by observing *ma'at*, help to maintain the order established by the gods through *heka,* but a special class is responsible for honoring and caring for the gods daily, and this is the priesthood.

The clergy of ancient Egypt do not preach, interpret scripture, proselytize, or conduct weekly services; their sole responsibility is the care of the god in the temple. Men and women may be clergy, perform the same functions, and receive the same pay. Women are more often priestesses of female deities while men serve as priests. However, this is not always the case as evidenced by the priests of the goddess Serket (Selket), who are doctors (both female and male), and those of the god Amun. The position of god's wife of Amun, held by a woman, will become as powerful as that of the king.

High priests are chosen by the king, who is considered the high priest of Egypt, the mediator between the people and their gods, and so this position has political as well as religious authority. Akhenaten's high priest is called Pa-Nehesy, the same as Phinehas of the Bible. The priesthood is already established in the Early Dynastic Period in Egypt (c. 3150 - 2613 BC) but develops in the Old Kingdom (c. 2613 - 2181 BC) at the same time as the great mortuary complexes like Giza and Saqqara are being constructed by the Sirian-Annanuki.

The original Sphinx at Giza plateau monument is built over the Ark of the Covenant to protect it. The Sphinx is designed replicating Annanuki heritage, having the head of an Annanuki warrior placed upon the body of a lion-like sculpture. The lion's body of the Sphinx is a symbolic tribute to a race of beings known as the Lyrans, who are instrumental in laying the early foundations of Annanuki culture. The image above is the Sphinx located on the Giza Plateau.

The Sphinx is constructed to serve as a fortification for the Inner Earth portal and also as a safe house and library for the storage of sacred records and texts. The Sphinx, body of a lion and the head of a man, represents 12,000 years between the age of Leo and the age of Aquarius when Earth will ascend back to Terra as is foretold in the prophecies. The pyramids of Giza represent male energy with the upward triangle. While ancient Lemuria is the opposite and has downward-facing triangles that represent feminine energy.

Types of Egyptian Priests

Hemet-netjer refers to female priests and hem-netjer to male priests (servants of the god). The priesthood is organized in a hierarchy, with the *wab* priests at the bottom and the high priest (hem-netjer-tepi, *first servant of god*) at the top. The *wab* priests oversee the temple complex and may assist with festival preparation in addition to doing necessary but somewhat routine activities.

The *hour*-priests are astronomers who keep the calendar, determine lucky and unlucky days, and interpret omens and dreams. There are the doctors, who are also priests, the *swnw* (general practitioner) and the *sau* (magical practitioner) who both combine medicine and magic. A *ka*-priest (also known as a *ka*-servant) is paid by a family to perform the daily offerings at the tomb of the deceased. See the next image of Akhenaten's high Priest Pa-Nehesy, carved statue in Egyptian Alabaster.

Akhenaten's high Priest Pa-Nehesy, carrying a Falcon-headed standard. The same as Phinehas of the Bible.

There are also *sem* priests who preside over mortuary rituals and conduct funeral services. They are the embalmers who mummify the corpse and recite the incantations while wrapping the mummy. The *sem* priests will remove the organs during the mummification process. They are responsible for the precise utterance of the spells that will guarantee eternal life to the deceased. The image above is of a statue of Akhenaten's high priest Pa-Nehesy/Phinehas. The image below depicts the same priest from the biblical perspective.

Just below the high priest is the lector priest (*hery-heb* or *cheriheb*), who writes down the religious texts, instructs other clergy, and recites the *authoritative utterance,* the *heka,* in the temple and at festivals. Although there is evidence of women serving in all other positions in temple life, there is no record of a female lector priest. The image below is a painting of Pa-Nehesy/Phinehas.

Priest Pa-Nehesy (Egyptian)/Phinehas (Biblical) grandson of Aaron.

The fact that there are no records of a female lector priest could be because the position is usually passed from father to son.

Often the high priest positions were part-time. Priests and priestesses were divided into *watches* and served the temple one month in every four. When their month of service was up, they returned to their regular jobs in the community, which was often of a mid-level bureaucrat nature. While they were in service, priests lived in the temple complex. They were expected to be ritually pure, bathe several times per day, and be on call for whatever was required of them.

Chapter 5

KEEPERS OF THE BLUE FLAME

There is conflict between Serres-Egyptian-Melchizedeks (Hebrew), Anu-Melchizedeks (Israelites), and Akhenaten, opening the portals of the underworld. This causes a closing to the Halls of Amenti, and guardianship of the Ark of the Covenant is transferred to the Hibiru Cloister (Hebrew). The Hibiru Cloister establishes the Essenes. Jeshua-9/Jesus (Arcturian) is later born into the Essene community at Qumran.

Following the death of Aye (Aaron/Ephraim from the Bible) (half-brother of Tiye) in 1348 BC, the Melchizedek Cloister Keepers of the Blue Flame became scattered throughout Egypt, being considered criminals of the state for their prior affiliation with Akhenaton. In 1309 BC, the Elohim plans for the opening the Halls of Amenti and the races for the mass ascension wave of 2012 AD.[59]

Channeled ~ 2019 *(Stacy/Shakinah) Semenkhkare/Sabatoth (Akhenaten's half-brother and Nefertiti's full brother) ~ son of*

Amenhotep III/Solomon and Sitamun, a priest of Ur, Blue Flame Melchizedek, and primary holder of the knowledge uses both light and dark energy and is a Keeper of the Blue Flame and member of the Serres-Egyptian Priesthood.

Keepers of the flame are headed by

- Primary Flame Holder = 3D Phaelopea High Priestess
- Inner Circle Flame keepers = 3D General Horemheb (army general)
- Semenkhkare/Sabatoth (physician and half-brother of Akhenaten and full brother to Nefertiti)
- Two hundred other members of the Blue Flame Melchizedeks

The Keepers of the Flame are responsible for assisting people who are ready to take the morphogenetic wave voyage in preparation for ascension. The Keepers of the Flame receive their infusion of 5D (fifth dimensional) frequency from one primary individual who has the genetic code that allows the Flame to be fully embodied as it passes through the Ark of the Covenant. That person is the Flame Bearer or the Staff Holder. The Flame Bearer activates the twelve-strand DNA package within their own body before being able to embody the Flame. This person incarnates with a support team of six fully activated twelve-strand Avatars (souls from the fourth Harmonic Universe).

There is conflict between Serres-Egyptian-Melchizedeks and Anu-Melchizedek/Israelites and Akhenaten, resulting in the opening of the portals of the underworld. This causes repercussions and the subsequent closing of the Halls of Amenti. Guardianship of the Ark of the Covenant is now transferred to the Hibiru Cloister (Hebrew).

From c. 1363 BC to 1362 BC the Keepers of the Blue Flame lead qualified Serres-Egyptians and others to the Ark of the Covenant at Giza, successfully ascending several thousand individuals not of Anu (Annanuki and Sirian hybrid Human) descent through the Halls of Amenti. The Blue Flame Melchizedek priests (Serres-Egyptians) continue the ascension of their people in secret. In this way, the original mission contract to establish the Law of One is to be fulfilled. However, when the portals are closed due to misuse, the souls that go through the Halls of Amenti are now fragmented. Some do not have this knowledge.

Semenkhkare/Sabatoth discovers that Akhenaton is using the Halls of Amenti, and so he, going against the advice of the other Flame Keepers, also continues ascension attempts for the Serres-Egyptian people. Semenkhkare/Sabatoth discovers that by using the D-2 portals, he is able to merge the individuals' consciousness with their anti-particle double and transmute their DNA. This is made possible by way of the passages of the Halls of Amenti and orchestrated without the use of the Staff or Blue Flame. However, these ascension practices caused incomplete ascensions. In an incomplete ascension or the splitting of light and dark, one has failed to address their own darkness.

Incomplete Ascension

There are two types of ascension that occurred historically upon Earth. One form of ascension leads to the development of a fourth dimensional biology and a *real complete ascension* to the next dimension; the other leads to the enhancement of an ever-increasing nonphysical field that inflates the souls associated without ascending the form (incomplete ascension).

In an incomplete ascension, the Light Body is constructed into an ever-increasingly large formation and united with many other light bodies of many other Humans, often in complex swirling energy flows of varying sacred geometry patterns. However, because none of the forms of the associated Humans have moved up in vibration in biology, as the ascent is launched, his or her body combusts, and the entire united Light Body collapses back upon the group, who then become ill and die.

False ascension inflates the thoughtform of combustion, as the form does not ascend, but rather combusts into a pile of ashes, and the combustions become increasingly incomplete with entire body parts such as heads, legs and arms left behind.

It could be said that those attempting to ascend their people were misguided by the false gods. Within six generations after the last false ascension, all remembrance of the DNA required to build this level of awareness in Human form disappeared from all Human genetic archives.[60]

In 1361 BC, Semenkhkare/Sabatoth is imprisoned by those who raised him for his knowledge of the Ark of the Covenant portal passage and ascension activities. Akhenaton and Semenkhkare/Sabatoth are among those of the Cloister

Melchizedek and Serres-Egyptian lineage that are now placed under the Templar-Axion Seal. The Templar-Axion Seal causes distortions in the DNA. For any future ascension activities, these individuals have to have their twelve-strand DNA imprint realigned before anyone can again ascend through the Halls of Amenti.[61]

Semenkhkare/Sabatoth left behind a legacy within which lives the hope of the Keepers of the Blue Flame. Horemheb and the Keepers of the Blue Flame keep the child's true lineage hidden and orchestrate a marriage between this child and Akhenaton's third daughter, Ankhesenenamun.

The Elohim intervene, the rod/staff are deactivated, and the halls of Amenti are sealed. The entry into the portal of the Inner Earth is sealed. The guardianship of the Ark of the Covenant is now transferred to the Hibiru/Hebrew Cloister races.

The Sphere of Amenti is a Closely Guarded Secret Since the Atlantean Cataclysm

With the assistance of the Sirian Council, Elohim, and HU 2 (5th Dimensional Earth, see image in chapter 10 Ascension - Definitions, *Universal Time Matrix, Twelve Time Fields in Fifteen Dimensions*) Pleiadeans, the Ur-Terranates form an agreement with several other races called *The Covenant of Palaidor*. The mission involves the creation of the Sphere of Amenti to allow open transit between Earth and Terra for beings possessing genetic codes that could endure portal transit. Those involved in this agreement are the Sirians, Pleiadeans, Ur-Terranates, Elohim, Lyrans, Ceres, Lemurians, and Atlanteans, who become known as the Palaidorians.[62]

The purpose of the Sphere of Amenti is to assist the reintegration of Earth's dimensional fields and to activate the twelve-strand DNA imprint in Humans. It is a race morphogenetic field, a Host Matrix (surrogate morphogenetic field or *form holding blueprint*) through which the Lost Souls of Terra may evolve and return home (see Chapter 10 Ascension).

Melchizedek Priesthood

The original Melchizedek Priesthood as it exists today was founded on the surface of Earth in c. 1490 BC in the area of Salem (Jerusalem) with the birth of Tuthmosis III (King David), a Nephilim (a Sirian-Human hybrid). He carries a patriarchal version of the Templar Creed, which allows knowledge of ascension and genetic protection to reach the Hibiru races. Tuthmosis III (King David) becomes known as King of Salem. As a result of the Templar Creed influence, Humans become lost to their purpose and are trapped within the patriarchal slant. The foundations for the modern-day Jewish religion are based upon the establishment of the Priesthood of Melchizedek among the Hibiru/Hebrew, through which the mystical studies of the original Kabbalah are organized.

Tuthmosis III, also known as King David, Templar-Anu, and son of Osiris and Isis, has a son with Sarai/Sarah named Isaac.

Amenhotep III is the great-great grandson of Tuthmosis III, Akhenaten's father. Amenhotep III dies in 1367 BC, the 39th year of his reign. Amenhotep's purpose for coming to Earth is to ensure the opening of the Halls of Amenti and to realign the morphogenetic field of the Anu (Annanuki and Sirian hybrid Human) races. Once the realignment of the morphogenetic field is aligned, souls may reenter into the Sphere of Amenti. Amenhotep III attempts to orchestrate ascensions for the Templar-Anu, Anu-Melchizedeks, and elected others of various races whose genetic codes are evolved enough to undergo this process and return to *Terra*.

Second Israelite Lineage Enters Back into Egypt via Yuya/Joseph

The four Armana Rulers, Akhenaten, Semenkhkare/Sabatoth, Tutankhamun, and Aye/Aaron/Ephraim, attempt to ensure the opening of the Halls of Amenti and to realign the morphogenetic field of the Anu-Melchizedeks and Serres-Egyptian-Melchizedek races (re-entering into the Sphere of Amenti). It is these races whose genetic codes are evolved enough to undergo the ascension process and return to *Terra*.

For five years, Akhenaten successfully trained and ascended thousands of people through the Halls of Amenti and 5D frequencies back to Terra (the first world) in secret. Akhenaton successfully practiced the rites of ascension among the Anu (Annanuki and Sirian hybrid Human) populations from c. 1367 BC to 1362 BC Although the general surface population of Armana saw him as neglecting his duties, he was on an important spiritual mission and helped those beings who possessed an active fifth DNA strand in their Genome.⁶³

However, the mission is thwarted due to Akhenaten's favoritism of his mother Tiye's Anu-Melchizedek people over the Serres-Egyptian-Melchizedek races, showing unwarranted prejudices. Tensions begin to mount between Akhenaton and the Ur Priesthood when he is instructed to begin ascending other individuals not of Anu lineage. He has broken his original soul agreement to assist the ascension of non-Anu lineage, and the Halls of Amenti are closed by the Priests of Ur, the guardians and gatekeepers of the time portal structures that link Earth to present-day Terra.⁶⁴ The image below is a gold funerary mask of Semenkhkare/Sabatoth, biological father to Jesheua-12/Tutankhamen.

Gold funerary mask for Semenkhkare/Sabatoth (Blue Flame Melchizedek).

Semenkhkare/Sabatoth secretly holds a pro-Amunist view, Kemetism, the worship of a few gods (Maat, Bastet, Anubis, Sekhmet, or Thoth, among others). Kemetistic worship generally takes the form of prayer, offerings, and setting up altars.

Semenkhkare/Sabatoth recognizes the existence of every god, and just like his son, Jesheua-12/Tutankhamen, is killed for attempting to bridge the Amunist (polytheistic, recognition of many gods and goddesses) and Atenist (Aten worshipers).

Semenkhkare/Sabatoth's reign lasts only a few days. Semenkhkare/Sabatoth is imprisoned as a traitor in 1361 BC by the Serres-Egyptian Priesthood at Thebes (with whom he was raised in childhood) and tortured for his knowledge of the secrets of the Ark of the Covenant, then executed in 1352.

Due to Akhenaten's mishandling of the secret knowledge, there are now divisions among the Elohim HU 3 (7th Dimensional Earth, see image in chapter 10 Ascension - Definitions, *Universal Time Matrix, Twelve Time Fields in Fifteen Dimensions*), the Sirian Council of HU 2 (5th Dimensional Earth, see image in chapter 10 Ascension - Definitions, *Universal Time Matrix, Twelve Time Fields in Fifteen Dimensions*), and the RA confederacy. Two primary groups evolve out of the original Melchizedek Cloister: Melchizedeks Cloister (Hebrews) and the Templar-Melchizedeks (Templar-Anu). The Templar-Anu (Melchizedek Cloister and Sirian A Annanuki) have a distinctly patriarchal slant promoting gender subservience and are not originally part of the Cloister Family. As a result of Templar-Anu influence, the controlling of women and the influence of a male elite begins. These two groups are now the *chosen ones*. The Melchizedeks

Cloister (Hebrews) and Templar-Anu have the special privilege of ascension if they follow the teachings of the Elohim's altered Templar Creed. At this time, the seed becomes infected, and the God force is seen as exclusively masculine—blocking other forms of worship, elitism, persecution, violence, and death.[65]

Timeline of Events Following the Confrontation Between Akhenaten and the Keepers of the Blue Flame

- Jesheua-12/Tutankhamen takes the throne at age ten in 1361 BC.
- Haremhab and the Keepers of the Blue Flame keep Jesheua-12/Tutankhamen's true lineage hidden and orchestrate a marriage between Jesheua-12/Tutankhamen and Akhenaton's third daughter Ankhesenamun (1360 BC).
- Jesheua-12/Tutankhamen rules for ten years (see Chapter 7) until he is killed at the foot of Mount Sinai while attempting to bridge the Atenist (Serres-Egyptian Melchizedeks) and Amunist (polytheistic, Anu-Melchizedek) beliefs of Egypt in 1352 BC.
- Aye/Aaron/Ephraim (the last of the Amarna kings) rules Egypt for four years from 1352-1348 BC.
- Army general Horemheb takes the throne from 1348-1335 BC. Abolishing the worship of Aten, Horemheb sequesters the Israelites and Akhenaten's followers into the city of Zarw.

Anu-Melchizedek and Serres-Egyptian-Melchizedek (Hebrew) Connections

Egyptian stele, Nefertiti (Serres-Egyptian-Melchizedek) mother of Jesheua-12/Tutankhamen/Joshua (Ye-ho-shua) son of a fish.

The genogram image below shows lineages for the descendants of Thoth, starting with Tuthmosis III and Sarai/Sarah.

Tuthmosis III

Descendant of Thoth, the Original Bearer of the Law of One, and holding Atlantean Knowledge.

Thuthmosis III (Templar-Anu) & **Sarai/Sarah** (Hibiru/Hebrew-Melchizedek)
Israelite Lineage Begins

Isaac (Anu-Melchizedek)

Jacob/Israel

Yuya/Joseph (Anu-Melchizedek) M Tuya (Serres - Egyptian Priestess)

Tiye (Anu-Melchizedek)

Tuthmosis IV M Mut Muya

Amenhotep III
Sitamun

Amenhotep III m Sitamun — **Amenhotep III m Tiye**

Semenkhkare/Sabatoth and — **Nefertiti** m **Amenhotep IV/Akhenaten**

Jesheua-12/Tutankhamen — **Princess Scota/Maritaten** (see Chapter 8) *Christianity & the Druids/Gnostics*

Genogram created by S. Ray, 2024.

Semenkhkare/Sabatoth and Nefertiti are parents of Jesheua-12/Tutankhamen (Joshua, Ye-ho-shua) son of a fish

Semenkhkare/Sabatoth is married to Scota/Meritaten (daughter of Nefertiti & Akhenaten) for three years.

Recent DNA testing points to Akhenaten and Nefertiti as parents of Tutankhamun. However, the biological parents of Tutankhamun are Semenkhkare/Sabatoth and Nefertiti. Due to the fact that Akhenaten, Nefertiti, and Semenkhkare/Sabatoth have the same father, Amenhotep III/Solomon, the results will show the family DNA in Jesheua-12/Tutankhamen remains

Anu-Melchizedek and Serres-Egyptian-Melchizedek (Hebrew Connections)

Egyptian Iconography, Princess Sit-Amun.

Eighteenth and Nineteenth Dynastic Periods

(Mothers to Egyptian and Israelite Lineages)

Sarai = Mother of Isaac

Rebecca = Mother of Jacob

Rachel = Mother of Joseph (Yuya)

Mut Muya (Daughter of sun god Ra, see Appendix E) = Mother of Amenhotep III and Sitamun

Sitamun = Mother of Semenkhkare/Sabatoth and Nefertiti

Nefertiti = Mother of Jesheua-12/Tutankhamen (Arcturian)

Starseed Lineages on Earth

Serres-Egyptian (Hibiru/Hebrew) = Melchizedek Cloister (Holding the Fifth Degree Code)

Melchizedek Cloister and Sirian Annanuki = Nephilim - Guardians of the Ark of the Covenant

Hibiru/Hebrew and Templar-Anu = Anu-Melchizedek (Israelites)

The Templar Anu run the hybrid program on Earth. There is tension from Enki/Enoch to protect the Human race from exploitation.

Chapter 6

FIRST EXODUS: EIGHTEENTH DYNASTIC PERIOD

Akhenaten leaves Amarna with his high priests the Levites, fearing for his life and forced into exile. Akhenaten exiles to Sinai (upper Egypt). Akhenaten is accompanied by a group of his followers, which included his uncle Aye/Aaron/Ephraim, Chief Servitor/second priest of Aten Phinehas, and other followers. Akhenaten is thirty-four as he leaves his throne at Armana following his abdication in 1361.[66] The image below is a stone statue of Aye/Aaron/Ephraim, also spelled Ay. He rose from the ranks of the civil service and the military to become king after the death of Tutankhamen, holding the throne for four years in the late fourteenth BC. The stele below is of Aye/Aaron/Ephraim, Chief Servitor/second priest of Aten, Akhenaten's uncle.

Stone stele of Aye/Aaron/Ephraim, Chief Servitor/second priest of Aten.

Akhenaten takes with him his brass serpent staff, a symbol of his pharaonic authority. See a depiction below of Akhenaten and his serpent staff.

Akhenaten/Moses and his serpent staff.

During this time, army general Haremhab and the Amunite priests devise a plan to take control of Egypt. It is believed that for a time, Nefertiti as Neferneferuaten takes pharaonic power at Amarna and shares coregency with her brother Semenkhkare/Sabatoth. After only a few days on the throne, Semenkhkare/Sabatoth is killed. In the midst of all the confusion, Jesheua-12/Tutankhamen takes the throne at nine years old and rules Egypt for ten years. After ten years of pharaonic rule, Jesheua-12/Tutankhamen is killed by Phinehas at the foot of Mount Sinai in Egypt, at age nineteen, and Aye/Aaron/Ephraim takes the throne of Egypt for four years.[67]

Aye/Aaron/Ephraim held the throne of Egypt for a brief four-year period in the late fourteenth century BC. Prior to his rule, he was a close advisor to two, and perhaps three, other pharaohs of the dynasty. It is speculated that he was the power behind the throne during his great nephew, Jesheua-12/Tutankhamen's reign. The image below is a Relief of Aye/Aaron/Ephraim and his wife Tey, receiving the gold of honor from Akhenaten. Multiple double-stranded shebyu-collars are draped around their necks.

Relief of Aye/Aaron/Ephraim and his wife Tey receiving the gold of honor from Akhenaten.

Horemheb Marries Nefertiti's Sister, Mutnezmet/Mut

Following an army rebellion, Horemheb seizes the Throne of Egypt, appointing Pa-Ramses and Seti as Vizers.

In 1348 BC, Horemheb (eighteenth dynasty) uses his military power to place himself as ruling authority of Egypt. Horemheb is known as the pharaoh of oppression. He orders the Israelites and Akhenaten's followers to the city of Zarw, which has been fortified into a prison. The Israelites are eventually cast out of all positions of power within Egypt by Horemheb and strongly encouraged to depart Egypt. The image below is a statue of Mutnezmet/Mut, Nefertiti's sister.

Mutnezmet/Mut, Nefertiti's sister.

Revolutionary Religious Changes in Egypt

Holleman (2016) supports the idea that Akhenaten's favorable relations with the Israelites and his love for Nefertiti resulted in his instigation of the revolutionary religious changes in Egypt during his six-year reign. Holleman believes this is why Akhenaten is later vilified and known as the Heretic King. Holleman compares the period of time that Akhenaten ruled Egypt with the current political and religious unrest in the US. In his book *The Prosperity Clock*, Holleman explains that the crisis period that the US is entering now has many similar features of the time during which Akhenaten ruled Egypt. The image of the Relief below shows Nefertiti with three of her daughters under the solar disk, Aten, eighteenth dynasty 1331-1334 BC.

Nefertiti with two of her daughters under the solar disk, Aten (eighteenth dynasty, 1331-1334 BC).

Second Exodus (Biblical Exodus–Nineteenth Dynastic Period)

During the reign of Ramses I, (1335 -1333 BC) and after 28 years in exile, Akhenaten/Moses travels back from Sinai into Egypt. Akhenaten, distraught over what he perceives as the failure of his earthly mission and the death of Jesheua-12/Tutankhamen, travels to Egypt to confront Pa-Ramses (Ramses I) and to claim his right to the throne. When Akhenaten is unable to persuade Pa-Ramses (Ramses I) of his rightful place as pharaoh of Egypt, Akhenaten leads the Israelite tribes, his Egyptian followers, and his friends the Midianites out of the Egyptian borders. Osman, (2005) supports the idea that Akhenaten is subsequently stopped and killed by Seti I (Rameses I's son). The Israelites now become nomadic and wander the area around Mount Seir in Edom for approximately 40 years. Subsequently, Ramses II campaigns wars throughout the land of the Shasu people, lasting from c. 1182–1151 BC. Once Egypt loses control of Palestine during the second half of the twelfth century BC, the Israelites, still living as nomadic peoples, begin to enter back into Canaan.[68] The map below shows the three time periods for Akhenaten's exodus, including exodus #1 when he traveled to Midian, exodus #2 when he traveled to Mount Sinai, and exodus #3 when he traveled back to Egypt to Goshen near Pithom. Pithom is one of the cities which, according to Exodus 1:11, was built for the pharaoh Ramses II, known as the pharaoh of the oppression. He used the forced labor of the Israelites. Ramses II was the builder of Pithom. He reigned from 1279-1213 BC. See Appendix F.

The Mysterious Death and Burial of Akhenaten

In 1907, a mysterious tomb was discovered in Egypt. Known as KV55, the tomb contained a variety of artifacts and a single body. Identification of the body has been complicated by the fact that the artifacts appear to belong to several different individuals. It has been speculated that the tomb was created in a hurry and that the individual buried there had been previously laid to rest elsewhere. In January 1907, financier Theodore M. Davis hired archaeologist Edward R. Ayrton and his team to conduct excavations in the Valley of the Kings in Egypt. The Valley of the Kings is an area in Egypt located on the West bank of the Nile River, across from the city of Thebes. Almost all of the pharaohs from Egypt's Golden Age are buried in this famous valley (Reese, 2010).

The image below is of the Valley of the Kings located in Egypt where the New Kingdom's pharaohs, including pharaoh Akhenaten (Moses), Jesheua-12/Tutankhamen, and pharaoh Ramses II, were entombed.

Valley of the Kings, Egypt.

Current day, Valley of the Queens, Egypt.

The famed Valley of the Queens is seen in the picture above. Despite its name, the rugged Valley of the Queens holds more than just the tombs of the wives of former pharaohs; it is also the resting place of several significant officials and their descendants. Nefertari, Titi, Khaemwaset, and Amenherkhepshef are among the approximately seventy tombs that may be found in the Valley of the Queens in upper Egypt, a canyon in the hills along the western bank of the Nile River.

Chapter 7

CHRIST CONSCIOUSNESS TWELFTH LEVEL AVATAR

Jesheua-12/Tutankhamun/Joshua

Jesheua-12/Tutankhamen is born to Semenkhkare/Sabatoth (Blue Flame Melchizedek) and Nefertiti (Serres-Egyptian-Melchizedek); both Essenes. Guardianship of the Ark of the Covenant portal passage is now in the hands of the Hibiru Cloister races. Reintegration of the Races into and Restoration of the Sphere of Amenti becomes the mission of the twelfth level, twelve-strand DNA Avatar Jesheua-12/Tutankhamen (Arcturian). The Azurites and Elohim (Lyrans) work together through the Melchizedek Cloister, establishing the Essene brotherhood about 1240 BC, which is originally designed to bring the undistorted Templar teachings of the Law of One back into manifestation on Earth. The Essenes who work with the Priests of Ur and the Azurite council are known as the Blue Flame Melchizedeks.

Jesheua-12/Tutankhamen Avatar child, the son of Semenkhkare/Sabatoth and Nefertiti (brother and sister) is brought to 3D Earth in order to help Akhenaten during a time when the *divine plan of evolution* is taking place. Akhenaten's life is being threatened by the Amunist priests, and he needs a successor to the throne. Jesheua-12/Tutankhamen's mission is to bridge the Atenist (Serres-Egyptian Melchizedek) and Amunist (Anu-Melchizedek) perspectives in an attempt to bring back the original teachings of the Law of One, through which Egypt could be unified and serve as a model for preparing the races for ascension.

In 1352 BC, seventeen-year-old pharaoh Jesheua-12/Tutankhamen is attempting to bring Akhenaten/Moses back from exile in Sinai. Jesheua-12/Tutankhamen is accused of *misleading* Akhenaten's followers. As a result, Jesheua-12/Tutankhamun is tortured and killed by Phinehas (Hebrew for Pa-Nehesy), an orthodox Atenite priest. Jesheua-12/Tutankhamen dies at the foot of Mount Sinai. See chapter 4 for more about Phinehas.

The teachings of Jesheua-12/Tutankhamen and Jeshua-9/Jesus are originally included in the manuscripts that become the Christian Bible but are distorted or edited entirely at various times to suit the needs of the power elite within the evolving political and religious circles. The original teachings of Jesheua-12/Tutankhamen and Jeshua-9/Jesus are also distorted and misrepresented through political and religious structures of various times. The teachings of Jesheua-12/Tutankhamen and Jeshua-9/Jesus and the Templar Melchizedeks become the primary foundations for the contemporary Jewish and Christian faiths. The Templar Melchizedeks (having a distinctly patriarchal slant due to ET distortion) create a primarily patriarchal religious structure.

The Jewish rabbis and priests did not acknowledge Jeshua-9/Jesus as their savior. In truth, Jesheua-12/Tutankhamen is the true savior of the Serres-Egyptian-Melchizedeks (Hibiru/Hebrew). Jesheua-12/Tutankhamen reenters the Serres-Egyptian-Melchizedek races' morphogenetic field into the Sphere of Amenti. Few people knew of Jesheua-12/Tutankhamen and Jeshua-9/Jesus' Blue Flame Melchizedek Essene ascension school, so the majority of the Jewish rabbis and priests did not realize that their foretold Messiah had indeed arrived.[69] Jesheua-12/Tutankhamen and Jeshua-9/Jesus intended to bridge the gap between the Anu-Melchizedeks (Israelites) and the Serres-Egyptian-Melchizedeks (Hibiru/Hebrew), bringing back the original teachings of the Law of One.

Jesheua-12/Tutankhamen and Jeshua-9/Jesus leave Earth by way of the Ark of the Covenant. The Ark of the Covenant is held within the body as the *Merkabah*, which is electrical in nature. Merkabah, also spelled Merkaba, is the electrical vehicle used by Jeshua-9/Jesus and other ascended masters to connect with and transport to the higher realms. *Mer* means Light. *Ka* means Spirit. *Ba* means Body. Mer-Ka-Ba means the spirit/body surrounded by counter-rotating fields of light (wheels within wheels), spirals of energy as in DNA, which transports spirit/body from one dimension to another. However, the ascensions that were attempted during the time of Jesheua-12/

Tutankhamen and Jeshua-9/Jesus were false ascensions leading to the fracturing of the soul and monad. Many ascended masters that we are familiar with today did not complete their ascension, leaving their body behind, which resulted in combustion and fission, sending the fractured pieces of their soul into Earth's etheric field. These fractured souls are trying to find their way home again. At this time, they are being removed from Earth as there has been a long history of manipulations and the harvesting of chi from unsuspecting Humans upon the surface of the Earth.

The Ark of the Covenant is resealed within the UHF bands of D-3 following Jeshua-9/Jesus' attempted ascension, awaiting the time when Earth's grid rises high enough in vibration to allow for the return of the Sphere of Amenti. Twelfth level Jesheua-12/Tutankhamen and the ninth level Elohim Avatar, Jeshua-9/Jesus are two Avatars who become consolidated and are known as the *savior of the races*.

Christ Consciousness, Buddha, and Rama

Jesheua-12/Tutankhamen and Jeshua-9/Jesus, Buddha, and the incarnation known as Rama were each direct extensions of the Godhead/Goddesshead of this Creation (RAMA) who did not travel through the distortion of our cosmos to take embodiments upon Earth. They had no relationship to either Sananda or Matreiya. The purpose of Lord/Lady Rama sending in extensions of him/herself to Earth was to see if (s)he could reverse the distortion within their own creation of their own accord.

Many may not understand that the lifetimes of such beings as Jesheua-12/Tutankhamen and Jeshua-9/Jesus, Buddha, and Rama were created through a collaboration of many souls who came together to co-create these particular lifetimes. In each of these incarnations, more than 300 souls were involved in varying capacities to bring forth their respective biological ascensions. Each of the 300 souls involved were from outside of the distortion held within our creation. Some of the souls incarnated into the form from birth or held the embodiment for certain portions of the lifetime, and some overshadowed the form until it ascended.

Both Jeshua-9/Jesus (Elohim Avatar) and his eleven disciples came together with the soul agreements to ascend as a group into the fifth dimension. The ascension of Jeshua-9/Jesus and his disciples would have required the same genetic alteration that many ascending initiates are currently proceeding through upon the Earth plane. These initiations would have, however, taken much longer due to the lack of photonic energy upon Earth at that particular time in history.

We believe that Jeshua-9/Jesus made contact with a priest in Egypt that would have allowed both him and his disciples to utilize the pyramids to bring forth their respective ascensions. The seven Kumaras, who by this time in history had such control of the Earth plane, prevented Jeshua-9/Jesus' ascension by adding Karma to his unconscious and causing him to manifest his own crucifixion. The Karma appears to be added to the unconscious planes of reality, and Jeshua-9/Jesus was unable to access these records to clear them fast enough to prevent his own annihilation.

The Manipulations of Earth (Channeled by Asur'Ana)

Six million Earth years ago (24 million Human years), Arcturian Humans caused an ice age in utilizing Earth to hold a group of poisons that the Arcturians required removing from their own solar system so that they could ascend. The Arcturians froze Earth deliberately to assure that such toxins would release slowly. Most of the poisons prevailed, although the snow melted and became embedded in the genetic structure of all living things upon Earth. One could say that such poisons, along with the associated ice age, caused a major fall in consciousness for all sentient species upon Earth thereafter.

Three hundred thousand Earth years ago (1.2 million Human years), Sirius chose to create ice shields suspended in Earth's atmosphere to create global warming and a return out of a severe ice age. Much like a terrarium, the ice shields held enough moisture and heat upon Earth's surface that the snow could melt, and Earth could return to a tropical Garden of Eden again. There were many freshwater lakes and ponds that formed as the ice melted following the formation of the ice shields. Sirian Human scientists, unaware of the poisons prevailing upon the land, seeded such ponds and lakes with freshwater varieties of dolphins and whales about 1.1 million years ago, after Earth had thawed out.

One remaining species of a rather pure genetic inheritance to such forms of whales and dolphins is the Manatee in present time. The Manatee was found to be the most peaceful and gracious of underwater species. Indeed, the Manatee retains a magnetic energy flow akin to the early dolphins and whales seeded upon Earth. It is through the Manatee that a blueprint has been carved for all whales and dolphins to ascend into that shall lead to a magnetic, peaceful, and gentle nature that resonates with Earth.

The dolphins and whales lived within the poisons that Arcturus had displaced upon Earth, as the poisons had merged with all waterways as the ice thawed. Over time and within 400,000 years, the whale and dolphin consciousness declined. The full consciousness that they had known had been lost as the poisons created genetic distortions within their brain. When a decline happens slowly and over time, it goes unnoticed. It has only been in piecing together their own genetic records that the dolphins and whales have come to understand how the eight poisons embedded in all things upon Earth affected their biology. The poisons created a slow genetic alteration in which the brain capacity declined, leading to an increasing nonconscious state of being.

One can liken a nonconscious state of being as a part of self that splits off and is no longer acknowledged by the rest of self. The split-off part of self separates as the genetic encoding associated is no longer used by the physical in the construction of future offspring. This split-off part of self is also known as the *unconscious*. It is through the unconscious that the dark have worked through in the Human-whale-dolphin dream to manipulate Earth into an extinction cycle.

The ancient Human history has been a mystery not only to Humanity at large, but also to Earth. For Humanity has existed within a separate dream from Earth since the original seeding of Humankind about 200,000 years ago. It was not until the Human holographic planes were opened several years ago in Earth's global ascension that the entire Human history could be assessed. It has taken much time to recompile the archives of information and history so that an accurate account of all occurrences could be available for the purposes of global ascension and Human ascension alike.

Ascension requires an accurate compilation of all ancestral experiences and Karma to clear the Karma at any given vibratory bandwidth to ascend. The souls in care of the Human dream had little interest in ascension, so accurate records of Human experiences were never kept. However, all occurrences were still recorded in the Human dream, but in a nonsequential manner. Instead of time occurring sequentially with all incidents recorded from beginning to end, records were recorded and found based upon emotional resonance. In so doing, all records of a certain nature were held in one region rather than sequentially through time.

In Human ascension, this translates into one region of the form holding all records for a particular type of experience. If the experience is excessively painful, the region can also be excessively decayed or scarred due to all the painful records compounded on top of one another in the same part of the form. As this is for the Human form, this is also for Earth. Earth's most painful records are recorded one on top of another in the Middle East primarily; however, there are seventeen other regions equally painful, most of which are currently under the water of our oceans.

As the holographic planes were opened, the bits and pieces of Human history not understood through record gathering in Human ascension could be filled in. For the holograms have recorded a sequential history of every Human life ever lived upon Earth. Opening these archives has therefore been very helpful, as it has allowed much that had not been known until now to become understood. In this light, Earth would like to share a recounting of Human history from both a physical and nonphysical perspective.

Understand that this is our history. History repeats itself unless one chooses to learn the associated spiritual lesson and then choose a different outcome. Ascending Humans are choosing to learn their spiritual lessons and create a new era of unity ahead. Earth, as a global vessel, is choosing to learn her lessons as a consensus reality. In so doing, the future is shifting now to allow for the birth of a golden era ahead rather than a repeat of the many disasters that have plagued Humanity and caused falls in consciousness upon Earth.

The Kumaras' Manipulation

As Buddha biologically ascended about 34,000 years ago, the Kumaras fully infected the genetic patterning of the Human form. This was not Buddha's fault. The genetic material that he embodied (much like Rama's incarnation and ascension) did not allow for the entire unification of the unconscious planes of reality. Through the unconscious plane of reality, the seven Kumaras altered the Human DNA to further manipulate and control Humanity.

As an ascending initiate moves through their initiations in the ascension process, the archives of genetic material previously inaccessible become accessible. During this process, forces of the dark can manipulate or distort the genetic blueprint.

This occurred during both Rama's and Buddha's biological ascensions during their respective incarnations. As a result, the Order of Dari have brought forth a corrected blueprint for the Human form in the ascension process that is devoid of the distortions and manipulations of the Kumaras or any other force of the dark that has prevailed upon Earth. These new records are sealed and only accessible by the Order of Dari at this time. This is simply to prevent further distortion of the corrected blueprint, for there are still those present upon Earth who would like to prevent any form of ascension whatsoever. This information is given to initiates as needed after they have passed each segment of tests in their own initiation process.

In addition to manipulating the DNA during Buddha's lifetime, the seven Kumaras sealed the pathway to the fifth dimension following Buddha's ascension such that no one has been able to ascend since. An aspect of Rama returned in the form of Jesheua-12/Tutankhamen and Jeshua-9/Jesus because not one of Buddha's disciples biologically ascended following Buddha's ascension, and Rama knew that something must have gone wrong.

Embracing the Light of Christ

Many wish to embrace the light of Christ or become the flame of awakening. In order to hold such a flame, every attachment that one has, everything that does not resonate with one's choice to ascend, must be left behind. In order to become the light, one must embark upon the journey within that is self-uncovering, moving into the inner landscape and placing the inner guidance one receives through their heart from their soul above all else.

We see that these thoughts are not new, for the man loved by all known as Christ spoke such thoughtform himself in his own lifetime. Christ spoke that one must leave everything behind to enter the Kingdom of Heaven, and this is indeed a great truth upon the Earth plane.

Leaving those behind that cannot ascend may be painful at first. Sometimes it is accompanied by guilt, sometimes by loss, sometimes by the feeling of a broken heart. As the heart mends, the loss becomes filled with the love of one's soul and God Goddess All That Is. One can also allow the nature kingdoms and the Source of All Sources to fill the emptiness in one's heart and fill it to the brim.

No one can describe the sense of freedom that comes from the transcendence. In the freedom, the heart opens and can be filled with more love and more light than before the transcendence. As this occurs, there is joy that flows through that is inexplicable in nature. Each death and rebirth cycle, which causes one to leave the next layer of attachment behind, is filled with wonder, filled with magic, filled with joy. In the joy, the light of Christ and the light of God Goddess All That Is shine bright for all to see. Christ ascended to 24 segments of DNA.

Return of Christ Consciousness

This is the fulfillment of the return of Christ that has been long spoken of. The return of Christ is the many who shall choose to leave everything behind and enter the Kingdom of Heaven through the act of ascension. In so doing, heaven shall be anchored upon Earth, and the light and unity once present upon Earth shall gradually be restored in the Human dance. Earth shall return and become once again the Garden of Eden with all species dancing in unity and harmony and as ONE.

This cannot occur unless some Humans choose to ascend, choose to transcend, choose to leave everything behind, and then anchor such light and love upon Earth. Know that those that enter such a kingdom of heaven are not alone, as there are many already underway in such an awakening. In due course, you shall find one another and create new communities of Humans that are unity-based. This shall be a true homecoming indeed.

Hold on to such a vision for your future. Intend it so. Allow a new dance, and new family of ascension to become your truth, your reality upon Earth. In so doing, you enter a new consensus reality where ascension is placed first and foremost in the minds and thoughts of all that join hands. In so doing, you shall not be alone, and you shall pull together, transcend together, change together, creating a new tomorrow for yourself and Earth, creating together a new manner of relating that is unity-based.

Such unity-based relations shall change everything upon your plane of reality. For all manners in which Humanity relates is separation-based, including the workplace, the marketplace, and the home. Such ascension-based communities shall explore and map-make a new manner of relating, but it will not really be new. Your ancestors related this way once long ago when they were unity-based. So you shall return and become that which your ancestry was long ago, together, hand in hand. The Source of All Sources and Mother Earth shall be a part of your new dance. The joy that shall be created and experienced is great indeed, both for Humans and for Earth.

The Source of All Sources' gift to Humanity is one of a new vision of a new tomorrow that is filled with love and joy, with Humans and children playing and dancing alike in harmony and unity again with all species upon Earth. Hold on to this vision and make it so. This new future only becomes possible if you intend it to be so, intend it into reality. Source shall fuel your journey home if you allow it, as Source shall stand at your side, through the tough times and into the joy again, bearing witness to your experience and guiding you each step of the way. Simply open your heart and ask, and Source shall be there for you. This is Source's gift to you.

More on Jesus Christ

We want to briefly discuss a number of the lies that the seven Kumaras have spread over Earth. There is a lot of material that is channeled that claims Jesus Christ rose from the crucifixion, but when Rama's soul records and the cosmic unconscious are examined, there is no evidence of this happening. We don't think that at that moment in his life, Christ was sufficiently advanced in his crystalline conversion to be able to ascend. Buddha's ascent took three hundred years. We think that because of the density of the Earth at the time of Jeshua-9/Jesus' incarnation, it might have taken him much longer.

It was also just discovered from the cosmic archives that Joanna, a woman, was actually John the Beloved, also known as John the Apostle, a disciple of Christ. Joanna went with Jeshua-9/Jesus and the disciples while dressing like a man. Because it would have been challenging for her to teach as a woman, particularly after Jeshua-9/Jesus' execution, Joanna covered herself in this way. Just before she passed away, Joanna also wrote the Book of Revelations. We point out that the ability to see into the future is a product of feminine DNA, and that material would most likely be funneled through a feminine form. In addition, Joanna represented the twin flame component of the soul embodied in the persona of Jeshua-9/Jesus and an extension of Rama. Despite their intense love for one another, their relationship was never completed since they accepted vows of chastity.

The Kumaras have spread numerous falsehoods concerning an ascension process that doesn't necessitate the transformation of the form into a crystalline cellular structure. As already mentioned, this is false ascension. The cosmic libraries show that since Lord Buddha's incarnation 34,000 years ago, no one has been known to rise from the Earth plane. We think that in order for the Kumaras to maintain their hegemony over Humanity, they holographically inserted false information into Human genetic memory. Every Human has records of every person who has ever lived on Earth, including Jesheua-12/Tutankhamen and Jeshua-9/Jesus, Buddha, and Rama, encoded in their own genetic material. For 34,000 years, the Kumara family has had unrestricted access to the genetic archives, allowing them to add whatever myth or falsehood they like.

It was also revealed recently that Jesus Christ was Sananda's incarnation. Christ was led by Sananda to his crucifixion. Given how painful it was, why would Sananda or any other red god participate in the Human dance once more after withdrawing long ago? In order to free himself and proceed to a different dance that more deeply satisfied him, Sananda entered the dance with the intention of driving Humanity toward extinction. The thoughtform of crucifixion is similar to extinction.

An increasing number of the red and white gods have manifested themselves within the last century. They have resumed performing the Human dance. The majority of people have believed that maybe they are here to elevate Humanity and usher in the Golden Era of Human existence. Earth is here to clarify that these are egotistical beings who only care about entirely extracting themselves from the dance so they can continue on somewhere else. They are not interested in changing Humanity. The red Grand Masters (large-headed Humans) would never have had their souls shattered and killed if the red false gods had any sort of interest in Humanity. Maybe they would have learned from the red Grand Masters instead.

These red false gods, however, have become extremely conceited and are incapable of learning anything. Because the red false gods are nothing more than an element of interference,

Earth has decided to eliminate them from the Human dream in order to facilitate the ascent of Humanity.

Crucifixion Karma

The Karma and death of 70 large-headed Humans added crucifixion Karma to all seven root races: African, Tibetan, North American Indian, South American Indian, Aboriginal (Lemurian/Australian), Inuit (Alaska/Mongolian), and Polynesian. The reason for this is that the 70 who died had interbred with all root races over time. This set up Humanity for an extinction cycle across all lineages and tapestry of ancestries. Extinction is associated with crucifixion and the belief that the spiritual path leads to annihilation rather than evolution and ascension home. As this Karma is transcended by enough ascending Humans, the extinction cycle Humankind has been upon can conclude, and a new era and day be born.

The crucifixion Karma we speak of is not associated with the life of Christ, for Christ's ancestry was primarily Anu and Anu slave at the time that he died. He had yet to access his ancient red ancestry that held the records of the Mahavishnu; it appears that long before this could occur, the crucifixion Karma associated with the destruction and annihilation of the slaves was triggered and Christ manifested his own death before he could ascend beyond it.

Christ was crucified due to the Karma of the Mahavishnu; Christ's ancestry went back to the large-headed Humans. Christ tried to stand in his truth and was destroyed for it. This pattern has played out again and again in history. If truth bearers were not destroyed in the physical dream through some travesty, they died of one disease or another over time. It is time to end the pattern of crucifixion. It is time to take Christ off the cross. The path of evolution need not lead to death; but in order for this to be so one will require releasing the Karma for being the savior and how the savior is crucified.

The Truth of Christ

What is the truth of Christ? That he was conned into being crucified, which led to another 2,000 years of warfare and bloodshed of the Human species as he was ascending at the time of his death, and the death and blood-shedding became world thoughtform as such. Mother Teresa as Christ's direct ancestor released much of this Karma in her lifetime, and she is honored as such. Mother Teresa now assists in the evolutionary process and testing of all initiates due to her own level of mastery of close to 5,000 segments or Bodhisattva level in her lifetime. And so, the purpose of Christ was fulfilled upon in Mother Teresa's life.

What was the purpose of Christ? To end the annihilation and birth the ascension movement for all of Humanity to attune to; Mother Teresa's life has allowed for the birth of the ascension movement in present time, and so one can say that Christ's purpose has been fulfilled upon. Now what must occur is the birth of unity, compassion, and honor as Mother Teresa exhibited it in each ascending master. As this occurs, one could say that the return of Christ to Earth has been fulfilled upon as a prophecy; however, it shall not come through a single individual but many carrying the flame of divine union of the Bodhisattva within.

Now it is understood that the red race carries parallel crucifixion Karma that must be released in order to see this through. One can also say that those of Annanuki descent time and time again have crucified the red race, which is a repeat of not only the era of the Anu but also the era of the pharaohs. This too ascending initiates must intend to transcend whether they be white, yellow, brown, or red in present time; for those who are ascending will each have ancestors associated with the era of the pharaohs in ancient times. As this Karma is released, a new type of leadership that has holographic wisdom may come forth and step into power.

Chapter 8

EGYPTIAN CHRISTIANITY AND THE DRUIDS/ GNOSTICS

Princess Scota/Meritaten (Akhenaten's oldest daughter) exiles to Scotland.

Princess Scota/Meritaten, the Egyptian princess and the oldest daughter of Akhenaten and Nefertiti, flees from Egypt and the chaos with a large following of people. The group first settles in Scotland and then travels to Ireland, where they are recognized as royalty by the Irish inhabitants. Princess Scota/Meritaten accepts a foreign prince in marriage in order to establish herself in her new country. A skeleton is found in Ireland in 1956, and the beads are dated to around 1350 BC. There are Egyptian faience beads on the skeleton that match the Egyptian faience beads found on Jesheua-12/Tutankhamen.[70] The next image is a clay statue of Princess Scota/Meritaten.

Clay stele, Princess Scota/Meritaten.

Princess Scota/Meritaten and her followers may be found in the myths of the people inhabiting Ireland starting in 1361 BC. The Tuatha de Danaan, the magical children of the goddess Danu, believed that Scota/Meritaten and her followers originally established the site of Terra, in the Boyne River valley, which is the ritual inauguration and burial place of the ancient kings of Ireland. Princess Scota/Meritaten and her people are generally regarded as the gods and goddesses of the Celtic tribes, and it is believed that their true origins date far back into prehistory Egypt.[71]

The exact location of Princess Scota's resting place remains a mystery, much like the particulars of her past, which are slowly being unveiled. As with many myths, a real person lends her persona and identity to the landscape of the land she became a part of, giving Scotland her name, giving the Celts an additional layer to their unique heritage that is unsung and still somewhat new in theory, as the truths of history do their slow unveiling.[72]

The Druids Teachers of Original Christianity

According to Osman (2004), the Gnostic sects formed groups in areas, including Palestine/Syria and Egypt, centuries before the start of the Christian era. The Nazarenes and the Essenes are two of these groups of Gnostics who lived for centuries prior to the start of the Christian era (p. 691). The Nazarenes and Essenes sought knowledge through spiritual experience. The term Nazarene is still used by Hebrew Jews today to identify Christians (p. 581).

To put it simply, the Irish Celtic tribes' priests are known as Druids, or Gnostics. However, merely mentioning that fact fails to capture the extent of their impact on Celtic culture. One branch of the Jewish people is the Druids. The terms Hebrew, Israelite, and Jew have all been misinterpreted. According to Osman (2014), Sigmund Freud, the father of psychoanalysis, was Jewish, Abram/Abraham was Hebrew, and Akhenaten/Moses was an Israelite. The Hebrews are referred to as Israelites until their return from the Babylonian Exile in the late sixth century BC.

There is a known connection between Joseph of Arimathea, Jeshua-9/Jesus' (Elohim Avatar) maternal uncle and the Druids (Gnostics). Rich metals merchant Joseph of Arimathea went to England to trade tin. On a number of these trips, Jeshua-9/Jesus traveled with his uncle to the Irish shore, near Glastonbury, where they encountered the Druids while strolling on the verdant English slopes. The Druids are often compared to the Pythagoreans of Greece and the Chaldean astronomers of Babylon.[73]

It is believed that Joseph of Arimathea established the first monastery at Glastonbury and built the first wattle church. An ancient Irish legend has it that Jeshua-9/Jesus himself traveled with his uncle from the Holy Land and helped in the building work. Finally, according to Druid legend, Joseph of Arimathea was buried somewhere at Westminster Abbey (London, England).

According to Sepher (2016), author and anthropologist, half of all Eastern European men are genetically related to Jesheua-12/Tutankhamen, born to Semenkhkare/Sabatoth (Blue Flame Melchizedek) and Nefertiti, who hold the fifth degree code of advanced genetic burdens for ascension. This includes 70% of British men, who hold the same genetic profile as Jeshua-9/Jesus (free of the DNA Seals of Amenti).

There are Gnostics in Alexandria and all around Egypt. The early Christians were taught by the Druids, or Gnostics, who spread their wisdom from Ireland to the East and beyond. This long-distance trip was made possible by commercial networks that connected Egypt and the United Kingdom. The Druids of the *Old Gaelic Order* later become the Gnostics in Ireland, practicing the original Christian worship of solar worship, well before the Roman Christians come onto the scene. The Gnostics did not maintain a hierarchy (Templar Melchizedek influence) within their mystery teachings. The image below shows early Christian symbols.

Early Christian Symbols

Osman, (2004)

In addition, the Gnostics denied that Jesus Christ was crucified and maintained that their savior lived many centuries earlier.[74] The Gentile Gnostics of Egypt and Alexandria have been called the Gnostics. The Gnostics assert that they have their own secret sources of information and reject the idea that Jesus Christ was physically raised from the dead, believing that he was raised spiritually. According to the Gnostics, Jesus Christ appears only in visions to selected individuals in various parts of the world.[75]

The first image below shows the serpent-pillar and the Hebrew prophets kneeling before Yahweh. A portrayal of Yahweh as the god of the Israelites. Notice the Hebrew Prophets kneel before Yahweh and how Yahweh's head curls around the base of a pillar. His body is that of a serpent. Notice the serpent head and body. According to Henry (2019), the Ark's missing piece (serpent power or Kundalini) has been found. This is not an isolated incident.

The second image shows a German Christian Gnostic Thaler, sixteenth century, linking the crucifixion of David's (Tuthmosis III, King David) ancestor, Jeshua-9/Jesus. See chapter 2, Mixing of the Races Begins.

The Hebrew Prophets kneel before Yahweh.

German Christian Gnostic Thaler, sixteenth century (Henry, 2019).

The Gnostics of Ireland, Scotland, and England believe that the symbol of the serpent represents the ultimate balance of knowledge, energy, and spirituality. The Druids, Atlanteans, Egyptians, people of India, and Asia worship the symbol of the serpent/dragon and believe the symbol represents metamorphosis (from serpent to a higher spiritual form). Over time, however, the sacred symbol of the serpent is demonized by Roman Christian influence.[76]

The Gnostics are a sect that opposes the Roman interpretation of Christianity and is a super-class of priests, teachers, healers, political counselors, and arbitrators among the Irish Celtic tribes. With the intention of defending Roman Christianity, Henry II invades Ireland. This invasion resulted in the persecution of Gnostics and 800 years of British control over Ireland. The Druids built the Newgrange burial mound in ancient Ireland during the Stone Age, illustrating the significance of sun worship and death rites to the pre-Irish people. Stonehenge (Sirian) is in almost perfect condition today and is only about 40 miles north of Dublin, close to the river Boyne. It is noted that the Egyptian pyramids (Sirian) are much the same age as the early Irish structures, both Irish and Egyptian cultures having early Sirian influence. The pyramids were used to launch the false ascensions.

Christianity starts to take on a hierarchical structure around 200 AD. At this point, in order to set themselves apart from the Roman Orthodox Christian Church, Gnostic Christians identify themselves as Egyptian Gnostics. The Gnostics hold that spirituality is a subjective experience and that all adherents of

Christ's teachings are equal. Higher knowledge is the result of self-knowledge, according to the Gnostics. A defeat of Gnostic Egyptians who practiced the Serapeum faith in Alexandria is subjugated by further tensions between the Orthodox Roman Church and the Gnostics of Alexandria. During this period, Julius Caesar (392 CE) destroys the Alexandrian library on the instructions of Bishop Theophilus I, who had outlawed the practice of ancient faiths.

The Alexandria library is originally founded in Egypt by Alexander the Great and the Egyptian Pharaoh Ptolemy I Soter in 283 BC. The library is modeled after the shrine of the Muses in Athens, Greece. It is the destruction of the Alexandria library that has kept the Egyptian origins of Christianity a secret for well over sixteen centuries.[77] Ancient records contained in the Alexandria library in Egypt bring together North Africa, Middle East, Central Asia, and India, providing ancient writings of the *knowledge* dedicated to the Muses and the nine goddesses of the arts. However, the Alexandria library is destroyed by Julius Caesar in 48 BC, which results in the lost knowledge. To trace the history of the library is to trace the history of Alexandria itself. Both were conceived by Alexander after he conquered Egypt in 332 BC. When Alexander established the city that bore his name as Egypt's new capital, he also made plans for a great library dedicated to the Muses. The image below is an artist's drawing of *The Library of Alexandria*.

Pencil drawing reproduction of the Alexandrian Library.

Chapter 9

JESHUA-9/JESUS ELOHIM AVATAR

Jeshua-9/Jesus-*Ben Joseph* (Hybrid Avatar) is born to Mary (Sirian) and an Arcturian ET father. Jeshua-9/Jesus is the reincarnation of (Jesheua-12/Tutankhamen) Joshua of the Bible.

Joshua or Jehoshua (Hebrew יְהוֹשֻׁעַ Yehoshuʻa) is the central figure in the Hebrew Bible's Book of Joshua. According to the Hebrew Bible, Joshua was one of the twelve spies of Israel sent by Moses to explore the land of Canaan.

The story of Jesus Christ, as it is known in contemporary times, evolved through the mythology the Elohim used to conceal the identity of their Avatar, Jeshua-9/Jesus and to perpetuate their patriarchal slant on the Templar Creed. The distortions of the true facts of history are used to protect the lineage of Jeshua-9/Jesus from political persecution, making it appear as if the Christ had no descendants, thereby allowing those descendants to remain obscured from the public view.

Jeshua-9/Jesus is taught from a young age by the Essenes at Qumran. The Essenes/Phoenicians (Khalu) are made up of a portion of the people from Atlantis. The original Essenes, the Khalu, give the Essenes their *secret knowledge*. The Kalu are still on Earth and are the guardians of the secret knowledge.[78] The name Essene comes from the word *Essa*, the Arabic name for Jesus Christ and the only word for Jesus Christ used in the Koran. *Essaioi* refers to *follower of Essa or Jesus*.[79]

Jeshua-9/Jesus is born into, brought up by, and taught by the Essene community at Qumran. The Essenes and Nazarenes are early Christian Gnostic sects who are the Keepers of the Covenant *believe in me and you shall have eternal life* and are an offshoot of the followers of Akhenaten/Moses who follow his Commandments.[80] The Essene community is a closely protected group that has separated from the Jewish and Jerusalem priesthood.

The Essenes believe they are the people of the *New Covenant* (eternal life through their teacher who would return). The Essenes' teacher is none other than Jesheua-12/Tutankhamen. Jeshua-9/Jesus is the reincarnation of Jesheua-12/Tutankhamun, who has returned. Jeshua-9/Jesus (Arcturian Hybrid Elohim Avatar) is a closely guarded secret. He is protected and educated by the Essenes at Qumran.[81] The Essenes produce and hide religious documents known as the Dead Sea Scrolls. The map below shows Jerusalem during the time of Jeshua-9/Jesus' incarnation.

Map of Jerusalem during the time of Jeshua-9/Jesus' incarnation.

The Discovery of the Essenes' Dead Sea Scrolls

The discovery of the Dead Sea Scrolls in 1947 at the Israeli occupied West Bank and our growing knowledge of the Essene community that produced them gives us one of the most important pieces of evidence for the diversity of Jewish life and thought during the time that Jeshua-9/Jesus is on 3D Earth. The Essenes have gained fame in modern times as a result of the discovery of an extensive group of religious documents known as the Dead Sea Scrolls, which are commonly believed to be the Essenes' library. Josephus uses the name *Essenes* in his two main accounts, but some manuscripts read *Essaion* (holding the Essenes in honor).

The Essenes are an ascetic Jewish group and a secret sect, who isolated themselves and did not publish about their community to the public. Belonging to the Essenes was no easy task, since all who were interested in joining pledged to keep the sect and its leaders a secret. Their stories are passed through community members by word of mouth, and it is very likely that people not belonging to this community had little to no knowledge of their existence during their lifetimes. The image below is of the Dead Sea Scrolls (Qumran Caves Scrolls) found in the Judaean Desert in 1947.

Remains of the *Dead Sea Scrolls*, Judaean Desert (1947).

The Dead Sea Scrolls (Qumran Caves Scrolls) found in the Judaean Desert in 1947 that inhabited eleven of the Qumran caves are ancient Jewish religious manuscripts known to have been written by the Essenes at Qumran. The scrolls contain significant religious literature describing the Essene community. The next image is a cave where the Dead Sea Scrolls were found near the ruins of Qumran, also known as Khirbet Qumran.

Ruins of Qumran (Khirbet).

The Essenes believe that their *teacher of righteousness* (Jesheua-12/Tutankhamen) has already lived and died at the hands of *a wicked priest (Phinehas)* and will someday return again. Their teacher of righteousness returns in the form of Jeshua-9/Jesus in 27 BC. The French scholar Andre Dupont-Sommer supports the idea that Jesus Christ of the Bible is an *astonishing reincarnation of the Teacher of Righteousness.*[82] Jeshua-9/Jesus is a closely guarded secret by the Essenes at Qumran. A light bearer during dark times, bringing spiritual initiation and hope to the people, Jeshua-9/Jesus is a wondering scholar and teacher for three years. He returns during the time of the Essenes at Qumran in an attempt to continue the work of Jesheua-12/Tutankhamen.

According to the Bible, Jeshua-9/Jesus' ministry begins when he is thirty years of age and continues for three years until he is believed to be crucified by the Romans. It is believed that he lived and died between 27 BC to AD 37 during the Roman rulers Octavian Augustus and his successor Tiberius. However, there are no records of Jeshua-9/Jesus' presence in historical accounts. He (Jeshua-9/Jesus) is not mentioned in any Roman contemporary writings during this period of history other than the references in the Bible.[83] In addition, the Talmud, a body of Jewish civil and ceremonial law refers to Elohim Avatar Jeshua-9/Jesus as *Balaam*. As Osman (2004) points out, the account of the resurrection and reincarnation of Jesus Christ (as depicted in the Bible) is in many ways similar to the account of Osiris in Egyptian mythology. The next image is a statuette of Osiris (c. 588 - 526 BC), featuring his characteristic atef (headdress) and shroud.

Osiris (c. 588 - 526 BC).

Jeshua-9/Jesus' mission is to teach the truth of the heart of God and to help others understand that they do not have to inflict pain onto others in order to have an understanding of each other. He comes as a guide to open access to spiritual understanding. He has brilliant blue eyes, tawny colored hair with streaks of the color of the sun at the roots. Jeshua-9/Jesus becomes *one with* those individuals who understand his message by taking these individuals into his light and vibration.[84] This is a profound spiritual experience intended to elevate those who are ready for a different dimension. This is a preparation for a larger understanding, helping us to remember who we are. The lesson allows us to transcend and know our spirits outside of our bodies; it is a gift of healing and white light. The next image is a painting of Jesus Christ the man, Jeshua-9/Jesus (unknown artist, 2019).

During the process of white light healing, there is a telepathic understanding, no exchange of words. Feelings, intuition, and spirit knowing are involved in this process—it is a transference of mystical knowledge. Jeshua-9/Jesus' message is to *find the light of God inside yourself* and to *see through your heart.*

> *The teachings of contemporary Christianity, though they provide a basic structure upon which social organization and spiritual initiation can be built, reflect little of the depth, content, or meaning of the original teachings of the Avatar Christ.*[85]

The Essenes at Qumran

Channeled ~ 2019 *(Stacy/Shakinah) I am a woman teacher in the Jewish Essene sect at Qumran. My family is originally from Asia Minor, current day Turkey.*

Between 1250 and 1200 BC the Sea Peoples/Khalu/Phoenicians (my ancestors) make their way from Asia Minor into Egypt and Canaan. Asia Minor is surrounded by the Black Sea and the Mediterranean Sea. Asia Minor is located between Christian Europe and Asia. Many ancient people such as the Hittites lived and occupied this land. The map below is Asia Minor during the time of the Jewish Essene sect between 1250 and 1200 BC.

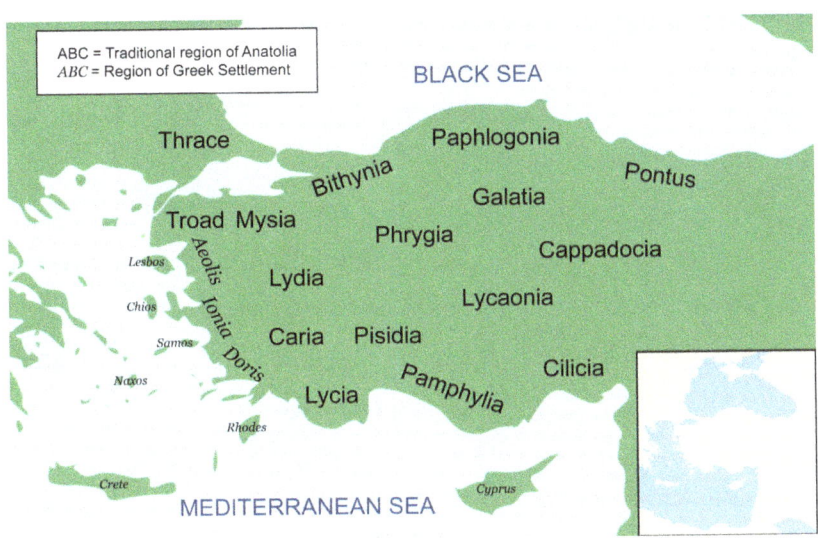

Asia Minor, in the years 1250 - 1200 BC.

The Essenes value women and treat them with respect and honor. *The Essenes have no restrictions and teach everyone according to their own desire and ability to learn.*[86] As a teacher and leader, a *way shower* for the children, I help the Essene children understand their own power through the knowledge of who they are as divine souls, teaching them to connect with the source of God within themselves. The children are taught that energy and frequency is in constant flux and that we are all part of a Universal harmonious whole. The Essene children learn the ways in which they will fulfill their own destinies through the patterns of creation and the basic laws to be followed. The children are taught that they are the holders of their own power, which is the essence of love. They are taught about the *I AM* presence of wholeness, abundance, safety, security, harmony, and the completeness that they are. The children are taught that separation from God is a myth. They realize and embrace the consciousness of oneness leading to the truth of who they are, light beings.[87]

Channeled ~ 2019 (*Stacy/Shakinah*): *Saint John the Baptist (Lyran, Arcturian, and Sirian) and I (Lyran, Arcturian, and Sirian) are cousins and are very close. He is my mentor, activates me, and is my teacher.*

Akashic Record Reading (Robin White Turtle Lysne 7/18/19): *Saint John gave you, Stacy/Shakinah, hope and faith helping you to rise out of doubt.*

Jeshua-9/Jesus teaches me about truth and healing. As members of the Essene community, the three of us (Jeshua-9/Jesus, Saint John, and myself) are taught the ways of ancient philosophies and healing techniques. The teachings include the Tree of Life and how to live in harmony with Universal laws. We are taught how to maintain our own power and faith in connection with the God that dwells within and outside of us. We are shown how our bodies and souls are connected to the sun and the earth. The sun represents masculine energy, and the earth represents feminine energy.

Saint John and Jeshua-9/Jesus are initiated by the priests of Ur at the Pyramid of Giza. This initiation is a ritual and a lesson in the cycles of death and rebirth. The concept of death and rebirth is demonstrated by the Elohim insert of Christ's resurrection. The lesson is that death of the physical body does not mean death of the soul and that the fear of death may be overcome. As we ascend out of our 3D Earth school, each of us will be initiated by breaking the death cycle and the reactivation of our fifth DNA strand. Prophesy tells us that the breaking of the cycle of death will occur when darkness covers Earth with the return of Christ or the return of the Law of One. This is when the fifth root race begins.

Jeshua-9/Jesus is Immanuel of the Bible

The Book of Isaiah refers to the birth of *a son and shall call his name Immanuel* (7:14). Isaiah used *alma*, a feminine word form of *alam*. Alma may be translated into the feminine form that relates to *the hidden one* or a feminine and hidden aspect of God. Immanuel is believed to be a synonym for Jesus Christ.[88] Jeshua-9/Jesus brings women before God on an equal footing with men and finds that women with their natural intuition and healing abilities are able to utilize his teachings. He teaches the metaphysical laws and how to use these laws to heal others. Jeshua-9/Jesus teaches us that the palms of our hands are the heart centers where healing takes place, and we can use our hands to heal others. Jeshua-9/Jesus' teachings and healings are radical for the time and are seen by the common people as miracles. Jeshua-9/Jesus believes everyone is equal, even lepers living in isolated colonies.

Jeshua-9/Jesus' mission is to help those in need and to teach about love and peace. He walks his own path and finds the Jewish priests (Templar-Anu influence) within the temple to be cruel and manipulative. The Jewish rabbis and priests of the time are following the ten commandments laid down by Akhenaten (Serres-Egyptian and Anu-Melchizedek), but due to the Templar-Anu influence are dismissive of the common people and subjugate women.

As the Romans dominate over Israel and Jerusalem, controlling the Galilean and Judean citizens through fear, Jeshua-9/Jesus acts as an instrument of peace by casting out fear with love. He is a gentle man who performs healings and miracles for those who need it the most; his message is to care for one another.

Jesheua-12/Tutankhamen and Jeshua-9/Jesus' message is one of peace and love, the same message in the prayer of Saint Francis:

> *Lord, make me an instrument of your peace*
> *Where there is hatred, let me sow love*
> *Where there is injury, pardon*
> *Where there is doubt, faith*
> *Where there is despair, hope*
> *Where there is darkness, light*
> *And where there is sadness, joy*
> *O Divine Master, grant that I may*
> *Not so much seek to be consoled as to console*
> *To be understood, as to understand*
> *To be loved, as to love*
> *For it is in giving that we receive*
> *And it's in pardoning that we are pardoned*
> *And it's in dying that we are born to Eternal Life*
> *Amen*

(Sarah McLachlan, artist songwriter)

Due to the work of Jesheua-12/Tutankhamen and Jeshua-9/Jesus, all races have been restored. The Halls of Amenti ascension portals of 2020 AD (fifth gateway)–2050 AD (seventh gateway) through the Halls of Amenti to Terra is back on schedule.

Three Elements of Christ Consciousness

Saint John (the Baptist), Jesheua-12/Tutankhamen, Jeshua-9/Jesus, and Saint Paul/Saul are the three elements of Christ consciousness incarnate into 3D Earth. The three elements of Christ consciousness bring lessons from the higher realms.[89] Saint John (the Baptist) lives until 29 AD. Jeshua-9/Jesus' ministry ends 30 AD. Saint Paul/Saul founds Christian Churches in Asia Minor and Europe, ministering to both Jewish and Roman citizens and dies in 64 AD. The image below is a painting of Saint Paul/Saul.

Painting of Saint Paul/Saul.

The Biblical Crucifixion of Jeshua-9/Jesus

Jeshua-9/Jesus is able to survive brutal treatment by the Roman soldiers prior to the crucifixion. He says *I lay down my life, that I might take it again. No man taketh it from me, but I lay it down of myself. I have power to take it again.*[90] It is Jeshua-9/Jesus' choice to end his mission at this time. The betrayals that transpire, the fighting, the mockery, and brutality are known events.

The dimensional veils are shattered after the biblical crucifixion, revealing to humans previously unknown facets of reality, and the common people of the period are clearly upset. This led to the uncertainty that followed the biblical crucifixion and to the dearth of historical narratives about the life of Jeshua-9/Jesus in Jewish and Roman history. There are many questions left unanswered pertaining to whether Jeshua-9/Jesus existed in the flesh. For instance, as mentioned in The Druids Teachers of Original Christianity, chapter 8, the Gnostics held that their Jesus Christ was a spiritual being who manifested to a small group of people rather than the actual Christ. Put another way, some people think that the Christ of Paul is a mythological invention that has been combined with the actual Jesus Christ, who did not exist. The writings of the Essenes and Gnostics made known by the discovery of the Dead Sea scrolls, which have reconciled the historical narratives of the lives of Jeshua-9/Jesus and Jesheua-12/Tutankhamen, are the exceptions to this confusion.

The resurrection of Christ is a Holographic insert by the Elohim. The Bible says that Enoch and Melchizedek were not born and did not die; they simply appeared and disappeared. I believe the disappearance and reappearance of Jeshua-9/Jesus happened in the same way—he left the 3D through the Ark of the Covenant and then reappeared through a Holographic insert by the Elohim.

Jeshua-9/Jesus' Bloodline—from the Line of David ~ Tribe of Judah

Jeshua-9/Jesus was closely connected to the Zealots (political faction) who planned to overthrow the Roman occupation. Below is a list of religious groups and descendants from the line of David, the Tribe of Judah, from oldest to most recent.

- **The Essenes** – among the Essenes were John the Baptist and Jeshua-9/Jesus (150 BC), Sun worshiped, Pythagorean thought, and profound healers. The Essenes were rigorously aesthetic, wearing simple white garb. The Dead Sea Scrolls were Essene documents.
- **The Valentinians (Roman Gnostic teachings)** – personal illumination over blind faith.
- **The Hellenistics** – the Hellenistics Claimed Jesus Christ did not die on the cross.
- **Nag Hamidi Scrolls (Gnostic)** – The Nag Hamidi Scrolls (Egypt), aka Gospel of Thomas.
- **Manichaeism (Gnostic Christianity)** – Manichaeism was a major religion founded in the third century AD by the prophet Mani (Persian Royal House). He claimed Jesus Christ did not die on the cross but instead was replaced by another man.

- **The Cathars** – the Cathars arose from the Manichaeans long established in France.
- **Arianism** – Arias lived in Alexandria (318 AD) and founded Arianism. He embedded Christianity in an essentially Judaic framework, displacing Roman Christianity by 360 AD. The Arians' claimed Jesus Christ was Human and was an inspired teacher.
- **Constantine** – Constantine was sympathetic to Arianism displacing Roman Christianity.
- **Arian Visigoths** – the Arian Visigoths became the dominant form of Christianity in France and Spain (Arian Christianity). Intermarriages between the Arians and the Franks resulted in the Merovingians.
- **Goths** – the Goths converted to Arianism from paganism, becoming Merovingians.
- **Merovingians** – the Merovingians rose to power during the fifth century (507 AD). Merovingian kings were closely connected to the Judean lineage.
- **Merovingian and Visigoth** – the Merovingian and Visigoth marriages resulted in Royal bloodlines.
- **Talmudic (Judaic)** – the Talmudic law was adhered to by Merovingians.
- **Visigoths** – the Visigoths later turned against the Jews and turned to Roman Christianity.

Chapter 10

ASCENSION

Blue Ray Starseeds

The Blue Ray Beings are an ultra-sensitive, empathic soul group like the Indigos that came from many different ascended planets and light realms to enlighten the genetic code of Humanity and raise the God Goddess All That Is consciousness on Earth. They are the lost ray of the Light Worker. Shekinah, a Hebrew word in the Language of Light, is a mentor of the Blue Ray. Shekinah is the lost aspect of the sacred Divine Feminine of Creation that is the embodiment of God Goddess All That Is. I am given the spiritual name Shakinah in 2020, during my contact with White Buffalo Woman.

The next chart explains dimensions eight to twelve and the spiritual law that is met during each level of mastery and transcendence to the next dimensional level of evolution or ascension.

DIMENSION	SPIRITUAL LAW
8th-12th Dimension	Service to the Cosmos (Infinite Love and Infinite Light)
7th Dimension	Service to All (Universal Love and Universal Light)
6th Dimension	Service to One (Divine Love and Divine Wisdom)
5th Dimension	Service to Love (Unconditional Love and Unconditional Wisdom)
4th Dimension	Service to Others (Unconditional Love, Compassion and Unity)
3th Dimension	Service to Self (Duality, Ego, Love, Divine Separation and Self Awareness)
2th Dimension	Service to Growth (Conscious, Sentient, Reproduction and Instinct)
1th Dimension	The Creation of Matter and Individual Consciousness

Dimensional levels of evolution.

The Evolutionary Path of Earth's Population Is on Schedule

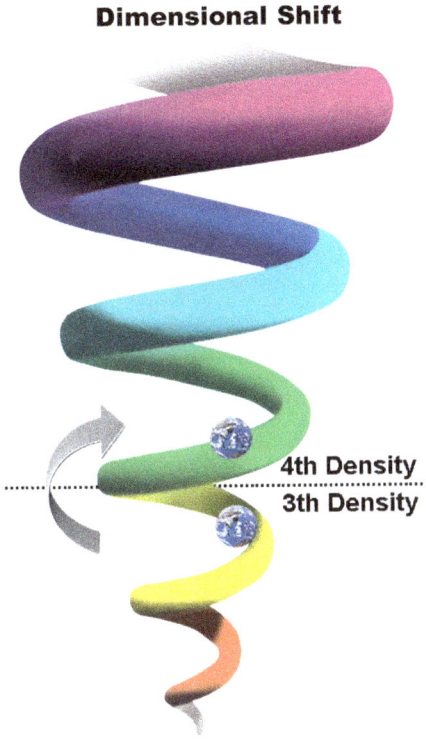

Earth's planetary shift.

Ascension is plural, meaning planetary ascension and personal ascension. Our Milky Way galaxy is currently ending a *major grand cycle*. This means that after 16 billion years, our galaxy has fully completed twelve processional cycles of orbital revolutions around the Great Central Sun, known as Alcyone Sun, which is located in the galactic center of the Pleiadean system. For us on Earth, the end of the grand cycle coincides with the completion of the 26,000-year minor cycle in 2012. In order for Earth to evolve into a 5D planet back to Terra, her frequency must be increased. This is a type of *reset* or reboot in order to start the next grand cycle of time (16 billion years). The levels of the Universe are dimensions and are involved in planetary ascension. The light spectrum represents the shifts in increasing frequency.

Earth's spiritual energy informs, transforms, guides, and directs our Human consciousness.

On December 21, 2012, Humanity successfully passed the marker of the 26,000 years spinning wobble around the sun. Meanwhile, our solar system entered into a new alignment with other planetary systems in the Milky Way galaxy. As a result, Earth has been receiving a new kind of light energy that activates the time capsules at the knolls and the nodes, spread throughout the world. The release of this light energy is stored Cosmic Energy that is preparing Humanity for more activations by forming a template that creates a protective shield around the Human cellular structure and the energy field of Human DNA. In fact, the light energy that Humans are currently receiving is far more powerful than ever before.[91]

It has been calculated that Earth moves from one astrological age to the next every 2,165 years. We are moving from the Age of Pisces into the Age of Aquarius.

Nelson (2015) notes that during the period between 2024 to 2027, there will be some rare and powerful astrological occurrences. At this time, Uranus and Neptune will line up, which happens every 30 years, providing the opportunity for calibration into a higher fourth and fifth dimensional frequency of resonance.

History tells us that with each astrological age, our religious symbols change. During the Age of Aries, the religious symbols were focused on the ram. The Jewish temples of the time practiced the sacrificing of rams on an altar of fire, which is discussed in the Old Testament of the Bible. During the time of Jeshua-9/Jesus, the Age of Pisces, the religious symbols centered around the symbol of a fish. Water Baptism becomes known at this time. The Age of Aquarius, an air sign, will be symbolized by a man carrying a pitcher of water. This involved the pouring of water into the air. The prophies from around the world within many religious beliefs foretell of 1,000 years of peace at this time. Our world will be united in Universal brotherhood through the practice of the Law of One. We are now moving into new Earth-based astrology signs.

According to Edgar Cayce's channeled readings, the date of Christ's birth is March 19, 4 BC. It is nearly precisely 2,030 years to the day of March 19, 4 BC, which is the spring equinox of 2026 that Nelson (2015) predicts as the second coming of Christ, worldwide brotherhood through the application of the Law of One. According to Nelson (2015), the sun and moon will darken when considering the prophecies regarding the return of Christ and a timescale for the Earth's transition into 5D (p. 1596). The Seventh Root Race and those who have ascended will comprise a new sort of Human body.

As we ascend and shift from 3D to 4D, we will be energetically shifting into the upper fourth dimension of reality. Earth's environment will comprise both 4D and 5D planes of existence. The challenge for Humanity is to ascend the biology by clearing Karma. This time ascension includes the physical body. The information for a complete ascension is being received through the Human heart center, Earth, nature, and the Tao within. The expansion of the heart/mind/body energic field is creating a process of opening up and clearing out of old patterns, energy, and blocks. This process of raising our frequency by integrating feelings, knowing, remembering, and the Human heart center, involves our higher self, the ancestors, Earth, and the Tao. How do we participate in the ascension process effectively? By loving ourselves and all of our history. What we put out into our world comes back to us. When our minds and hearts are connected, great things happen.

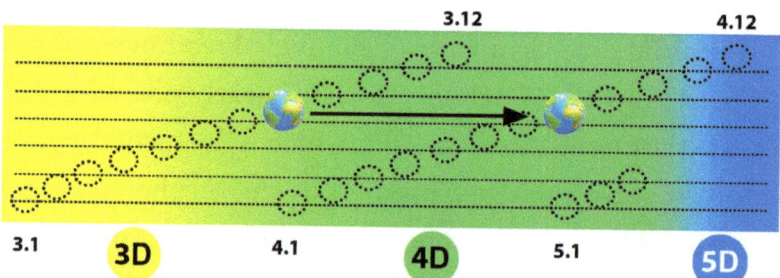

Earth will shift from the upper overtones of the 3rd dimensional frequency band (3.8) by spiralling upwards into the upper overtones of the 4th dimension (4.8)

Timeline for Ascension

It is a regenerative form that will be strong enough to withstand the rising vibrations and heat of the coming 25 years of global ascension ahead, allowing such Humans the ability to live to witness the birth of the new golden era. The list below indicates the timeline for ascension.

- The Ark of the Covenant begins a twelve-year descent of the Blue Flame in 2000.
- The opening of the Halls of Amenti in 2012.
- The release of the Sphere of Amenti directly into the D-2 Earth core morphogenetic field creates mass fifth DNA assembly in Humans in an attempt to help Earth with her ascension into 5D in 2012.
- The Seventh Root Race (Rainbow family of living light) and their Cloister have merged upon Terra, 2012.
- The fifth DNA strand is activated for those individuals passing their spiritual tests, and through the Sphere of Amenti portals, transmit 5D frequencies into the bio energetic fields of Earth.
- Terra merges into higher frequencies, the seven-to-twelve dimensional frequency DNA bands are activated and a molecular restructuring of the Humans physical and energic body occurs, realigning the original 12-strand DNA pattern.
- The practice of conscious evolution, cellular clearing, and DNA activation and transmutation is taking place, 2015.

- The Human bio-energetic field is directly connected to that of Earth. This progressive acceleration started in 2000 when the Human body began to receive energy infusions triggering a rapid release of the crystallized thought patterns stored in the cells and triggering rapid DNA activation, assembly, and expansion of consciousness, 2015.
- The energy of cellular activations will then indiscriminately alter the existing order of energies, which will manifest as energies moving through the bio-energetic field of the body and the consciousness. The ultimate outcome of these cellular activations is a restructuring of our body and the propulsion of consciousness and life drama into a higher level of peace, harmony, health, and order 2015.
- Earth entered the first star gate of the Great Central Sun in the year 2018.
- Earth attained 3,000 DNA segments in the physical in 2019. All nations have begun the ascent to 1024 segments of DNA.
- The 1.1 million Bodhisattva children are anticipated to enter the world in the coming 25 years that began in 2019.
- All incoming children are anticipated to enter the world at 3,000 segments beyond 2019.
- Poisonous thoughtform is being removed with the focus of anchoring the regenerative paradigm and a focal point in the global ascension of Earth in the year 2020.

- In 2022, Earth entered the great Central Sun Dream at 90%.
- Fewer crop circles in 2022. Crop circles are generated as the magnetic pulsations of the Great Central Sun Dream catch upon radioactive plates under Terra's surface. The radioactive plates have been a project for Terra to dissolve such that there is free flowing energy from end to end or all the way through Terra's core.
- The fact that there are fewer crop circles in the recent years is a sign that the radioactive plates that were generated in nuclear testing in the era of Atlantis are beginning to dissipate. Into the future, there may be no crop circles at all as all radiation under her surface has been dissipated in full; therefore, this is a positive sign of ascension.
- Terra entered two additional Star Gates in 2022, with the possibility of a third toward the end of 2023.
- Children were born in all nations at 3,000 DNA segments in 2021 and will number 800,000 DNA segments global wide by early 2023.
- Births at 6,000 segments shall begin in 2023; the more ascending children born, the stronger the movement toward equality and unity that shall likewise be born in all Human nations.
- War music for all kingdoms will be completed; as the war Karma is released as of the autumn of 2023, the war music will be diminishing global wide in all dreams and as a result.

- Overall, 10% of all births were Bodhisattva in vibration beginning in late 2019 and into 2020, 10% in 2021, 15% in 2022, 15% in 2023, 20% in 2024, and 30% by 2026.
- Beginning in 2018 and through 2027, the first wave of Bodhisattva level births will enter the world at 6,000 segments.
- It is anticipated that this shift shall be accomplished by 2026, and that after this time, electrical pulsations shall begin to rapidly dwindle.
- Cleansing begins. The times of cleansing shall begin roughly in the 2026 to 2028 timeframe for all silica-based life forms.
- It is anticipated that by 2028, there will be little radioactive radiation emanating from the Solar Sun.
- In 2028, the vibration of the Human species shall be high enough to introduce the first Mahavishnu level infants, and children will begin to be born with 15,000 segments of DNA.
- Beginning in 2028 and through 2033, the first wave of Mahavishnu-level births shall enter the world at 15,000 segments.
- Galactic Alignment will continue until 2032.
- Earth and those ascending with her are due to release the Karma for non-ascension completely by 2030 and for those ascending heralding the birth of a new dream ahead and the sustenance of magnetic flow within our structure and upon Earth and a new dream ahead.

- Melting ice caps and shorelines under water in the northern and southern hemispheres are anticipated to be commonplace by 2030.
- By 2030, four years will be pressed into a single year.
- By 2033, there will be little remaining electrical flow upon Earth. This is in preparation for entering the skin of the Photon Belt in 2048, at which point no electricity or radiation must be present upon Earth or in our solar system.
- World global peace by 2032 to 2033.
- Humanity will be freed from the dominion of the false gods, they will return to their creation of origins by 2033, and the most destructive of the false gods will no longer be present in any Human upon Earth.
- It is estimated that by 2034, Humanity may have created world peace among all nations, and that the real trauma and focus will be upon the many plagues and diseases associated with those who are unable to ascend and are leaving physicality. As this occurs, the next cycle of Grand Master energy flow will be fully in swing, and the new golden age will be born thereafter.
- Each species upon Earth is ascending their forms into a healthy enough version to withstand entry into the Photon Belt of the Great Central Sun. This is anticipated to occur around 2048, and as some of each species survives this transition, each shall be assured a future presence upon Earth along with an ability to ascend to the next dimension and ultimately home to the Tao.

- A new age of peace, unity, and abundance shall unfold for all kingdoms including Humankind, 2043.
- As the Pleiadian dream (Annanuki) is Karmically removed from Earth, there shall be enough harmony and holographic flow in the Human dream for entrance into the Great Central Sun in 2048.
- Entry back to the Great Central Sun, anticipated in 2048.
- Terra is on course to enter the Great Central Sun Dream in full around 2046 to 2048 at her current pace of global ascension.
- As ascension continues into 2050, all foreign DNA will have been removed from Human births.
- By 2060, it is anticipated that little electricity will be able to be harvested from water or the land as a result.
- When the release of fission Karma occurs in 2025, there will no longer be any fission-based threads to cause either nuclear annihilation or another false ascension leading to combustion among the Inner Earth Humans, dolphins, or whales.
- The Pleiadian dream and pyramidal flow is on target to completely collapse as Terra enters the new dream in full around 2046 to 2048.
- Terra is destined to enter this new dream in full in the 2046 to 2048 timeframe.
- Vegetation and algae: primary food source for all kingdoms upon Earth, 2052.
- There shall be no non-ascending Humans remaining upon Earth, 2053.

- By 2056, it is estimated that all of Earth shall exist in no time.
- All electricity will be removed from Earth, 2123.

A New Astrology for a New Earth

Earth is moving to a new Astrological system that is founded upon unity-based Universal archetypes. The Universe is made up of eighteen solar systems, of which Earth's Sun is also a part. All solar systems revolve around your Universal twelfth dimensional Universal Sun and in so doing, create an eighteen-year cycle that Earth was once a part of.

Each solar system anchors a particular archetype that is unity-based for not only Humankind but also all species upon Earth. Earth has anchored the necessary alterations along with your solar system to again partake in this eighteen-year cycle beginning in the year of 2019 and moving on into the coming eighteen-year period ahead.

As of 2019, the new astrology has been defined and embraced by Earth and all species therein. Ascending Humans are also embracing this new astrology and new unity-based archetypal patterning. See images below for assessing ascending astrological archetypes.

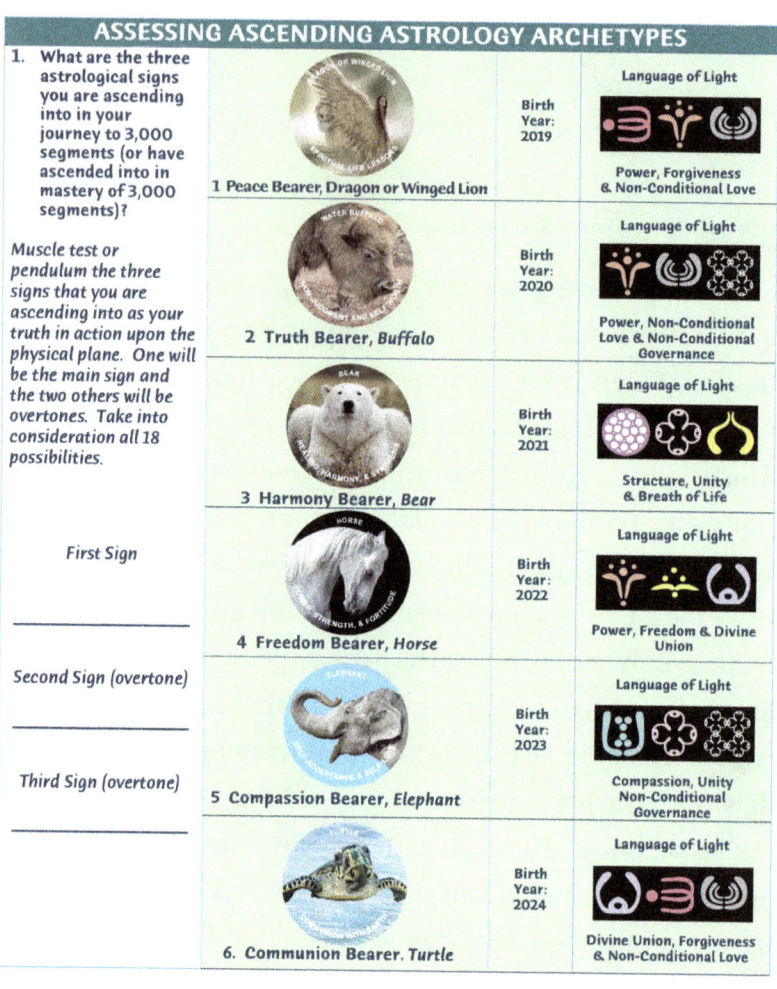

Assessing ascending astrological archetypes, original image modified S. Ray, 2024.

2. Which Language of Light tones are present more than once when all three signs are taken into consideration?

The Language of Light that appears 2 or 3 times when all three signs are assessed gives one an idea of the dominant Language of Light tones that reflect one's truth in action.

_____

_____

_____

3. What preoccupations would be useful given your truth in action?

What preoccupations would be good given your new astrological signs?

_____

_____

_____

Assessing ascending astrological archetypes, original image modified S. Ray, 2024.

4. What are the three additional signs that you are mastering to Bodhisattva level evolution? Fourth Sign _____ Fifth Sign (overtone) _____ Sixth Sign (overtone) _____ 5. Which Language of Light tones appear many times when all six signs are taken into consideration? _____ _____ _____ 6. What preoccupations would be useful given your overall truth in action? _____ _____ _____	13. Communication Bearer, Wolf	Birth Year: 2031	Language of Light Freedom, Unity & Breath of Life
	14. Divine Union Bearer, Swan	Birth Year: 2032	Language of Light Divine Union, Structure & Freedom
	15. Ascension Bearer, Tiger	Birth Year: 2033	Language of Light Forgiveness, Power & Non-Conditional Governance
	16. Evolution Bearer, Fox	Birth Year: 2034	Language of Light Divine Union, Non-Conditional Love & Non-Conditional Governance
	17. Evolutionary Truth Bearer, Antelope	Birth Year: 2035	Language of Light Structure, Compassion & Power
	18. Fulfillment Bearer, Porcupine or Kookaburra	Birth Year: 2036	Language of Light Power, Freedom & Breath of Life

Assessing ascending astrological archetypes, original image modified S. Ray, 2024.

Although one's birth year for the sign that one has been born under will not be reflected in this piece, one is altering their astrology through ascension to reflect a new truth-in-action that is unity-based and entering this new astrological influence.

Therefore, one's birth chart ceases to have as much meaning because a new pull of forces that are Universal in size begin to direct the dance more fully the further one ascends. One enters in full the new unity-based Universal astrological chart upon completion of Mahavishnu-level evolution (15,000 segments of DNA embodied).

Humans are used to archetypes that are solar in nature and polarity-based. For example, the current astrological signs each have positive and negative characteristics. Furthermore, some signs are predisposed to warfare or harmfulness in the life dance if the appropriate makeup is present in the rest of the chart. This is not so with the new archetypal patterns. In essence, the new archetypes are harmless and unity-based.

Birth Chart Reversals

In ascending to Bodhisattva, one's solar birth chart reverses fully, and one experiences the opposite to whom and what one has known oneself to be from birth for a time thereafter. For many upon the spiritual path, reversing their birth chart is a great gift in the ascent to Bodhisattva. Many spiritual aspirants chose to be born at a particular time with birth charts of extreme difficulty to teach one about the vital lessons of compassion in action. As a result, for many attaining Bodhisattva, life alters from difficulty and strife to greater ease and joy thereafter.

Through continued ascension beyond Bodhisattva to Mahavishnu-level evolution, the polarity reverses yet again, and the opposite of one's early life and life as Bodhisattva cancel each other out, coming yet again to the middle road, or a new dance of greater unity within. At Mahavishnu-level evolution, one integrates the opposing forces of the opposite solar birth chart and completes with this form of solar astrology in full, entering a new dance founded upon unity-based Universal astrological influences and forces thereafter.

Moving Out of Polarity-Based Astrology

The current astrology is solar in nature and was designed to govern the slave race with a limited genetic structure of only 5,000 segments as incubated by the Annanuki. It was also designed to keep one subordinate to those in power and unable to evolve out of slavery. The seeded race, on the other hand, was always governed by a unity-based Universal astrology, until they too fell to 5,000 segments or lower in vibration in the many falls in consciousness of the Human species. Then in the fall, the red race too fell under the solar astrology that had the effect of causing them to experience parallel limitation to the incubated slave race. One's ancient red ancestors therefore remember much about this ancient astrology.

One may wish to bring such knowledge forward now and intend to move into this new system in this lifetime. In so doing, one will enter a state of unity and anchor heaven upon Earth in one's own life dance and expression in this lifetime. For this is the fall from the Garden of Eden that has been written of. Humans fell from unity and a unity-based astrology into separation and a polarity-based astrology anchored by a limited group of Pleiadians to direct an even more limited slave race.

This ultimately caused the red race to fall into the dance of polarity of extremes or *fall from grace*. It is the extreme experiences of polarity that make life upon Earth in Human form an unpleasant experience for so many. Unity-based thought is not filled with polarity, but rather is founded upon the middle road or path between the two diverse poles. Therefore, Humans attaining Mahavishnu will be vastly different from their two strands of DNA past self in this incarnation.

There are many Bodhisattva children to be born in the years ahead that shall ascend to Mahavishnu in their early life dance, and many Mahavishnu children to be born after 2027 in Earth's estimation. The new astrology shall bring to consciousness the nature and expression of such children entering the world beginning in the calendar year of 2019. Therefore, this piece is also dedicated to the incoming Bodhisattva and Mahavishnu children. May there be many of such births, and may such children lead Humanity Home to a new dance of unity, Unconditional Love, and peace.

Unity-Based Truth and Astrology

Each ascending Human is moving toward embodying one of the following eighteen new astrological symbols as a reflection of their *truth in action* as an ascending master. Each truth in action is based upon three notes of the first ten upon the scale of the Language of Light; by the ascent to 3,000 segments of DNA, the first note is embodied; by 5,000 segments, the second note is embodied; by 7,500 segments or Bodhisattva, the third note is embodied by 15,000. All three notes are equally weighted within the field allowing for the truth-in-action to be reflected in the day-to-day life of the Mahavishnu-level master. It is also as all three notes are evenly represented in the field that one exits the old astrology and enters a new unity astrological system in full, one that surrounds the pull of eighteen solar systems around our twelfth dimensional Universal Sun.

The language of light notes are the foundation of a new unity-based thoughtform that pulls one increasingly under the influence of the new Universal astrology the further that one ascends. Ascending initiates may wish to muscle test which of these ten notes they are embodying first, second and third in their ascent to Bodhisattva. Know that the notes may change as one moves closer to Bodhisattva in vibration due to more clearly defining one's biological inheritance.

Eighteen New Astrological Signs for Bodhisattva Children and Ascending Masters

As three of the notes or tones are woven evenly in one's field, a whole new Human nature emerges. Know that the birth of those under these eighteen new astrological signs actually began in the year 2019. In 2019, Earth allowed 500 Bodhisattva children to be born global-wide. Most were born either to mapmakers or have grandparents who are mapmakers. Some others yet are mapmakers themselves that gave birth to such Bodhisattva children. These 500 Bodhisattva children are the first to be born in the Year of the Dragon, which began in 2019. All children born in the same calendar year will have the same birth sign under this new system of astrology.

One will note that this type of system is reflected in Chinese Astrology, which is based upon year of birth rather than month of birth. Chinese Astrology was designed this way as Buddha remembered enough of the ancient astrology to derive a new system. This new system shortened the eighteen original birth signs of the Universal system of the ancient red nation Humans to twelve signs, causing the red race related to Buddha to fall under a distorted system that blended the old Universal astrology with the solar astrology anchored by the Annanuki.

This system gave birth to a new system altogether currently known as Chinese Astrology. This also was a reflection of the time that the red race related to Buddha fell under 5,000 segments and therefore came to require such a new system as they fell from grace or out of unity.

It has been documented through the global ascension of Humanity that during Buddha's ascension, the genetic archives were opened, and the false intervention stripped the Human species of genetic information. Therefore, Buddha's ascension caused another fall without his awareness. Sad, as the consciousness of Buddha did not know what had transpired, and the souls that directed his ascension have recently returned to Earth to repair what was done as they hold Karma with Earth as a result.

Like so many ascensions that were beacons for the false intervention manipulations, Buddha was used. So it has been uncovered in most ascension that occurred during the time period preceding Buddha about 30,000-40,000 years ago. Buddha was the last of a line of red ascensions, each of which stripped the Human species until the red race fell en masse to under 5,000 segments and into another solar influence of polarity-based astrological influences.

At this time, the red indigenous races are ascending en masse. Many within their own nations have already attained Mahavishnu or higher in vibration. Asur'Ana has witnessed such ascensions amongst the Hawaiian nation. It is most magnificent to behold, and the red race is repairing themselves en masse of their own fall in consciousness. As it is for the red race, so it may be for all Humans that choose to ascend at this time in history. We are moving to a new way of being and returning to the joy and unity once known in each of our ancient ancestries. May this come to be so for all Human-wide.

Eighteen Birth Signs for the New Astrology Ahead

Each birth sign is related to a species of both the land and aquatic realm. These new signs can be thought of as new archetypes that the Human species shall ascend into over time. For those that pursue their personal ascension in this lifetime, one will live to experience the birth of these new archetypal patterns within one's own life expression. For those that choose to create ascending communities, one will draw such new archetypal patterns into the community. Each may wish to muscle test which sign that they shall fall under as they attain Mahavishnu-level of ascension.

Understand that ascension is not an easy journey, nor is what one discerns as one's truth necessarily accurate as one continues to ascend. Often ascension brings about the opening of ancient ancestral Karmic records that one has no knowledge of in present time. As such information is retrieved and reintegrated, one's truth in action and sign may therefore change. So be not attached to what you may ascertain today, as it may change as you continue to evolve.

Earth's Ascension Process

Planetary ascension refers to the modulation of Earth's energetic system passing into a higher frequency (raising vibration) and a *cleansing process*. Our bodies are connected and anchored to Earth's Ethereal body. For this reason, we are also passing into a higher frequency, raising our vibrations, and cleansing our etheric bodies and Chakra system. This is true for all living things on Earth. Our life force energy is connected to Earth as a result of the force energy that was supplied to us during gestation through food and water. Our physical and ethereal bodies are connected directly into Earth's energetic particle system. Therefore, during the transition back to the Great Central Sun Dream, a shift occurs. Earth will reach her next top frequency band and will overlap to the next highest dimension that creates a gateway to that density. Therefore, our ascension involves increasing the vibration of our crystalline DNA that leads to a biological ascension. In this way, we remain vibrationally anchored to Earth as she enters the Great Central Sun Dream once again as she returns home to the Tao. Increasing our frequency is available through the Law of One (Christ consciousness), a set of practices of unity consciousness, loving ourselves, loving others, and service to others.[92]

As an ascending population, we will find ourselves in a new time cycle upon Terra/Earth. Terra is Earth ascended to the fourth dimension and Gaia is Earth ascended to the fifth dimension. The population who does not catch the first morphogenetic wave will continue on into their own first Harmonic Universe time cycle (dimensions 1, 2, and 3). The ascension of Earth is foretold in spiritual stories and is known as the *Return to the Garden of Eden, Man's Ascension to Heaven,* and the *Coming of the Fifth World* in the Native American beliefs. Our spiritual traditions have been attempting to prepare us for this for over a million years. Our fifth world race will escape aging/disease and will carry the full twelve-strand crystalline DNA. Many but not all of our current ET visitors are our Seventh Race relatives from Terra. The name for Earth, Terra, is Earth ascended to the fourth dimension, and the name for Earth, Gaia, is Earth ascended to the fifth dimension. [93] Unity Consciousness is outlined in the next image.

Unity Consciousness

- Humanity living upon Earth operating together in the same positive polarity,

- All people experience the same higher frequency,

- The solidarity of global consciousness working in harmony, unity and collaboration in accordance with the whole,

- The synergetic union of human consciousness in harmonious cooperation,

- Humanity as a collective force living by the Law of One,

- Group consciousness, cooperative, shared materialism, worldwide alliance, and love.

Upon Ascension of the Body

In the past, Humans had the opportunity for a life review upon death (astral identity and projection of consciousness). During bardo, the soul becomes aware of its own pre-incarnation agenda as the veils created by the confines of the physical genetic codes are lifted. The DNA Seals of the Arc of Amenti aka The Seal of Amenti (7-D Seal) and the Axion Seal led to the implementation of the restricted genetic codes. The realization of one's own pre-incarnational purpose signifies the fulfillment of The Covenant of Palaidor. As a result of the fulfillment of The Covenant of Palaidor, mapmakers can now access the Arc of the Covenant, the Universal Tribal Shield, the Shield of the Arc (12D shield), and their own unique planetary keys. Resulting in access to the Arc of the Covenant, the Universal Tribal Shield, the Shield of the Arc (12D shield), and our own unique planetary keys (see chapter 2 - Into Egypt: Pyramid of Gizeh: The Seal of Amenti (7-D Seal) & chapter 3 - *The Axion Seal aka Templar-Axion Seal*). The soul then chooses the next living experience most appropriate to its own evolutionary path that may include a life purpose, life lesson, and life school.[94] However, due to the ascension process and those mapmakers who have forgiven ancestorial Karma, the life review is available before death.

Bardo Review Now Possible Before Death

So, what is bardo really? There are many ancestral threads of Karma that we activate as the physical vessel (the body) grows in the womb. There are many lessons. Lessons are very personal to each life dance. All Humans that pass from physicality enter a long period of bardo where they review their lives with the possibility of understanding the spiritual lessons that they were learning in the experience. This offers Humanity a broader perspective of the dance of life other than extreme right and wrong and the possibility of forgiveness to be born.

Bardo (life review) and all ancestral planes were severed from the Human physical planes and red nation Humans lost their connection to the nonphysical. However, the ascending mapmakers have forgiven massive amounts of Karma. As a result, the bardo (life review) and ancestral planes have been restored and are now present within all Human backgrounds. This means that those ascending may review their life while alive on Earth and clear the Karma consciously, rather than waiting for death for a bardo review.

Ascension Process

Akhenaton and the priests of the Blue Flame practiced the opening of the Halls of Amenti. However, the full frequency patterns of the Sphere of Amenti may only be transmitted through Earth's grid during the periods of dimensional blending that occur four times in each 26,000-year cycles. Akhenaton was able to open the Halls of Amenti and orchestrate ascension for those individuals who had the fifth DNA strand imprint, but he could not release the Sphere of Amenti directly into the D-2 Earth core morphogenetic field to create mass DNA assembly and ascension.[95]

As Earth progresses forward, there will be divisions in the population. In 2024, four of the six Silent Avatars will be brought to Earth in preparation for the passage into the particle pulsation rhythms of the D-4-time cycle. They are called the Silent Avatars because their identities, religious affiliations, and geographical locations will not be disclosed to the public. These four Silent Avatars are born with their DNA strands fully active (seven to twelve dimensional frequency bands). Their purpose for incarnating onto Earth at this time is to realign the Human DNA imprint and ensure Earth's grid stability by holding higher dimensional frequency in their bio-energetic fields as the Sphere of Amenti opens into Earth's morphogenetic field. As their respective soul essences pass through the Sphere of Amenti, the frequency bands carried in their energetic essence will purge mutations from the Human DNA imprint, allowing DNA strands two to seven to realign with the original twelve-strand DNA pattern. The identities of the four Silent Avatars will not be revealed until there is a mass practice of peace and an awareness of the Law of One (Christ consciousness), a set of practices of unity consciousness, loving ourselves, loving others, and service to others.[96]

When the Seventh Root Race (Rainbow family of living light) have their seventh to twelfth dimensional frequency DNA bands activated and the energetic grids of Earth and Terra reemerge, this will mark the fulfillment of The Covenant of Palaidor. This will represent the coming of the Fifth World, the Native American legend that is often referred to as the Warriors of Rainbow prophesy (see Appendix G).

The coming of the Seventh Root Race is also described in the Bible: 1Thessalonians 4:16-17, *For the Lord Himself shall come down from heaven with a commanding shout, with the voice of the archangel and with the blast of God's Shofar, and the dead in Messiah shall rise first. Then we who are alive, who are left behind, will be caught up together with them in the clouds, to meet the Lord in the air, and so we shall always be with the Lord. Therefore, encourage one another with words.*

The Edgar Cayce readings describe the DNA changes that will take place during our ascension: So as He (Christ) gave,

I leave thee, but I will come again and receive as many as ye have quickened through the manifesting in thy life the will of the Father in the earth.[97]

The return of Christ or the return of the Law of One will come again and be received by those who have done the work of ascending the biology through the works of a complete ascension, by those who have red root race DNA and are part of the Seventh Root Race.

The Bible and the Cayce readings talk about a change that is to take place. The description of being *caught up* (revive or make alive) or *quickened*. I believe this is a description of the 7D–12D frequency bands being activated and a molecular restructuring of all aspects of the body, realigning the original twelve-strand crystalline DNA pattern.

The more souls that assemble the fifth DNA strand, the quicker the Earth grid begins transmitting 5D frequencies into the bio energetic fields of the planet. Our work as a collective is to support each other and Earth by reducing pollution, nuclear waste, war, and other environmental harm that will make this process easier. This process will be aided by our capacity to sustain crystalline and high-frequency DNA; this can be achieved through the use of spiritual teachers, healers, ascension therapies, creative arts, meditation/prayer, inner child work, ego detachment exercises, grounding, physical exercise, emotional release, journaling, conscious breath, deep tissue massage, Karmic clearing, and by raising our Kundalini energy.

Definitions

Amarna is the modern Arabic name for the site of the ancient Egyptian city of Akhenaten, capital of the country under the reign of Akhenaten from 1353 -1336 BC.

Amenti: Duat (pronounced *do-aht*) (also Tuat and Tuaut or Akert, Amenthes, Amenti, or Neter-khertet) was the realm of the dead in ancient Egyptian mythology. The Duat was the region through which the sun god Ra traveled from west to east during the night and where he battled Apep.

Amunism (Kemetism, polytheistic, Anu-Melchizedek): The worship of a few gods (Maat, Bastet, Anubis, Sekhmet, or Thoth, among others), but recognize the existence of every god. This worship generally takes the form of prayer, offerings, and setting up altars.

Annanuki: Those who Anu (Pleiadian and Lyran) sent from heaven to Earth.

Archons: Gnostic for rulers of reality.

Ascension: Ascension in its basic spiritual or mystical sense may be thought of as the highest state of Man (Humanity). It is the expansion of awareness. It involves the realization of being one with the Creator and all of creation.

Assyrian: The **Assyrians** are a people who have lived in the Middle East since ancient times and today can be found all over the world. In ancient times, their civilization was centered at the city of Assur (also called *Ashur*), the ruins of which are located in what is now northern Iraq.

Atenism (Serres-Egyptian Melchizedek): Atenism, also known as the Aten religion, the Amarna religion, and the Amarna heresy, a religion in ancient Egypt founded by Akhenaten/Moses. As a result, there was an Amunist priesthood.

Chakra system: The Chakra system is a complex network of energy channels connecting energetic wheels and is mapped throughout the whole body, much like a spiritual nervous system. There are seven main and biggest Chakras that are found running alongside the spine.

Consciousness: Consciousness at its simplest is *sentience* or *awareness* of internal or external existence.

Covenant of Palaidor, Ark of the Covenant: The Ark of the Covenant is a Time Portal passage between Earth and the Andromeda Galaxy that was created 840,000 years ago by Guardian Races. It was used to store and protect the Sphere of Amenti until the Sphere could be returned to Earth's core. The Ark will directly impact the course of our evolution for the next ten years.

Dimensions: Dimensions are a means of organizing different planes of existence according to their vibratory rate. Dimensions are arranged in base rate wave lengths. The length of the base wave form is changed at each dimensional level. Each dimension has a certain set of laws and principles that are specific to the frequency of that dimension.

El Shaddai: Hebrew and one of the names for the God of Israel.

Electromagnetic energy: Electromagnetic energy is a form of energy that can be reflected or emitted from objects through electrical or magnetic waves traveling through space. Electromagnetic energy comes in many examples, including gamma rays, X-rays, ultraviolet radiation, visible light, microwaves, radio waves, and infrared radiation.

Elohim: The first light manifestation of the Emerald Order are Solar Rishi, Blue Ray orders of Elohim, and Oraphim that direct support to the Guardian Founder Races in the lower Harmonic Universe and are supporting GSF liberation and the continued spiritual evolution of Humanity toward Ascension and the Law of One. The Emerald Order of Elohim seeded the Anuhazi Feline Elohim races through the Lyran Twelfth Stargate in the fourth harmonic Universe, on Aramatena. The Elohim emerged from the Lyran founders and are the first forms created in the second Harmonic Universe.[98]

Energetic field, or energy-field: The spiritual energy produced by a particular living being.

ET, Extraterrestrial: Extraterrestrial refers to any object or being beyond the planet Earth (terrestrial).

Galactic Center: The Galactic Center, or Galactic Centre, is the rotational center of the Milky Way. It is 8,122 ± 31 parsecs (26,490 ± 100 ly) away from Earth in the direction of the constellations Sagittarius, Ophiuchus, and Scorpius where the Milky Way appears brightest. It coincides with the compact radio source Sagittarius A*.

Halls of Amenti: The halls of Amenti is a time portal passage that holds the race Blueprint field that would allow the fragmented Angelic Human souls to re-evolve back into original divine blueprint.[99]

Hall of Records: The Hall of Records is an ancient library referenced by Edgar Cayce to lie under the Great Sphinx of Giza, which is in the Giza pyramid complex.

Harmonic Universe Terra: The Universal Time Matrix is comprised of five density levels that each holds three dimensional holographic fields within them, or groups of three Spectrum of Frequency that manifest as platforms of consciousness perception and expression. Each of these density levels are organized into a trinity of dimensional reality fields, and each of these reality fields are also called Harmonic Universes or HU.[100] See next image for Universal Time Matrix, Twelve Time Fields in Fifteen Dimensions.

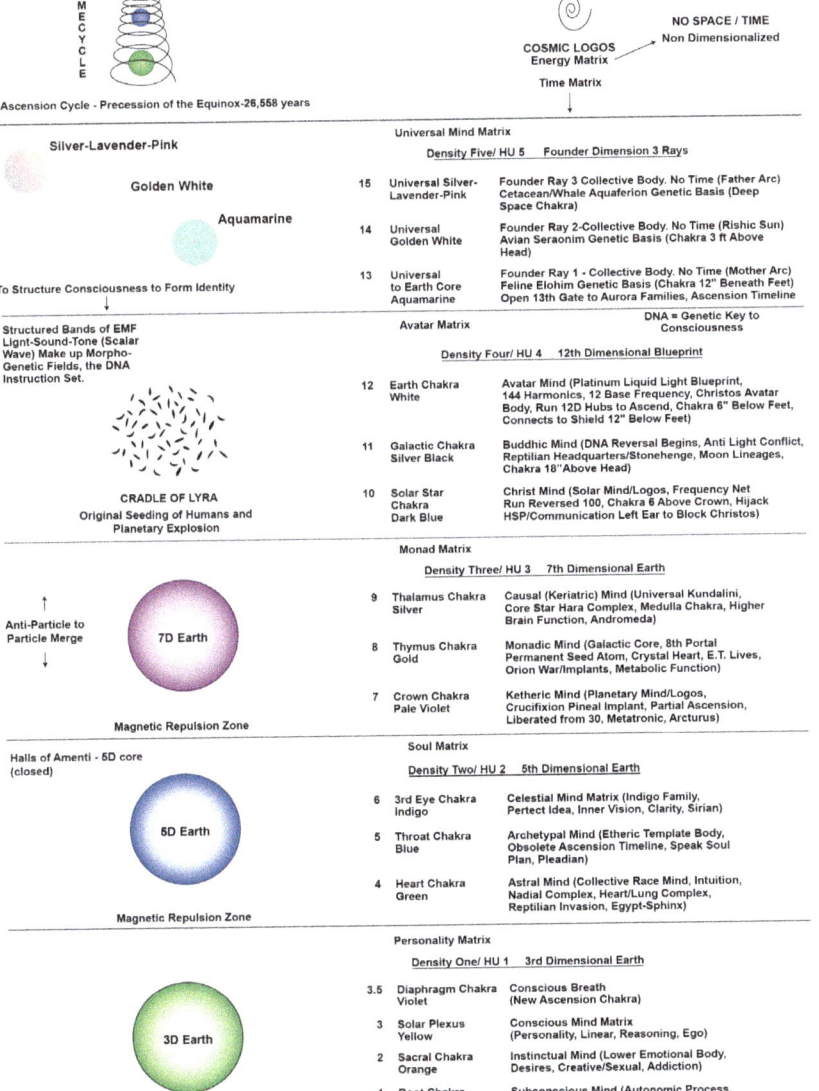

Universal Time Matrix, original image modified by S. Ray, 2024.

Harmonic Universe 1 (Earth): The Harmonic Universe 1 is one of the planets formed from the fragments of Terra (Universe 2) following the misuse of power and the implosions within Terra's planetary grid. As a result, she was expelled from the Great Central Sun, and this is how Earth came to exist outside of the Great Central Sun. As Earth exited, she was a twenty-fourth-dimensional star that split into 24 separate vessels, shattering much like a mirror, and created the constellation of a dragon within the space between.

Harmonic Universe 3 (Lyrans): The Harmonic Universe 3 is the main original Lyran-Elohim Humanoid races that are committed to the Law of One and Service to Others through krystic ideology. The Lyran-Elohim are supervising the Sirians to host the seeding of 12-strand DNA genetics on the 5D planet Terra. These groups involved in this seeding and DNA rehabilitations are called the Lyran-Sirian High Councils.[101]

Hibiru/Hebrew People: The Hibiru/Hebrew People are a Cloister mix of Hibiru/Hebrew and Melchizedek (advanced genetic burdens for ascension).

Jesheua-12/Tutankhamen: Jesheua-12/Tutankhamen rules Egypt for ten years (see Chapter 7) until he is killed at the foot of Mount Sinai while attempting to bridge the Atenist (Serres-Egyptian Melchizedeks) and Amunist (polytheistic, Anu-Melchizedek) beliefs of Egypt in 1352 BC.

Jeshua-9/Jesus, from the Bible: Also, the ninth level Elohim Avatar Jeshua-9/Jesus born to Mary and an Arcturian ET father.

The Jesus Christ of the Christian Bible, whom we have come to know.

Joshua (or **Jehoshua** (Hebrew: יְהוֹשֻׁעַ *Yehoshuʻa*): Joshua is the central figure in the Hebrew Bible, the Tanakh. His name was **Hoshea** (עֹשֻׁוהַ): The son of Nun, of the tribe of Ephraim, but Moses called him Joshua (Number 13:16), the name by which he is commonly known.

Nun /ˈnʊn/ (Hebrew: נוּן Nūn, *Perpetuity*): In the Hebrew Bible, the Tanakh, Nun was a man from the Tribe of Ephraim, grandson of Ammihud, son of Elishama, and father of **Joshua** (1 Chronicles 7:26–27).

According to the Tanakh, **Joshua** was born in Egypt prior to Exodus (aka, Jesheua-12/Tutankhamen).

Kemetic: Kemetic followers worship a few gods (Maat, Bastet, Anubis, Sekhmet, or Thoth, among others), but recognize the existence of every god. This worship generally takes the form of prayer, offerings, and setting up altars.

Mesopotamia: Mesopotamia is a historical region of Western Asia situated within the Tigris–Euphrates River system, in the northern part of the Fertile Crescent, in modern days roughly corresponding to most of Iraq, Kuwait, the eastern parts of Syria, Southeastern Turkey, and regions along the Turkish–Syrian and Iran–Iraq borders.

Melchizedek Cloister: The Melchizedek Cloister holds the fifth degree code, establishing the Essenes. The Melchizedek's have been the genetic hosting race. Because we are coming to the close of a Root Race end cycle, their tour of duty with Earth is coming to completion. This allows a time of review and pause for genetic rehabilitation and integrative healing for the Twelve Tribes. This is an alignment to the Mother's heart quintessence, to be rebirthed into the Creatrix field. This is the Mother ark and her rehabilitation of the Blue Ray and the *Sophianic* Body. The Holy Mother is progressively returning to reclaim and restore her creation, advanced Godhead technology included in the Ark Zone Blue Ray architecture that is modifying the planetary grid to transmit levels of the Sophianic Female Coding.[102]

Milky Way Galaxy: The Milky Way Galaxy is the galaxy of which the sun and the solar system are a part, and which contains the myriad stars that create the light of the Milky Way.

Mount Sinai (Arabic جبل موسى Gebel Musa): Mount Sinai is located in the middle of the Sinai Peninsula, Egypt, and rises 2,285 meters above sea level. The mountain is a sacred site for Jews, Christians, and Muslims.

Morphogenetic field: In the developmental biology of the early twentieth century, a morphogenetic field is a group of cells able to respond to discrete, localized biochemical signals leading to the development of specific morphological structures or organs.

Multidimensional frequency: Multidimensional frequency or multidimensional modulation (MD modulation) is modifying or multiplying an MD signal with another signal that carries some information or message. In the frequency domain, the signal is moved from one frequency to another, sometimes through the zero-point frequency.

Nephilim: The Melchizedeks Cloister and Sirian Annanuki Human hybrids.

Pleiadean system: The Pleiadean system also known as the Seven Sisters and Messier 45, are an open star cluster containing middle-aged, hot B-type stars located in the constellation of Taurus. It is among the star cluster nearest Earth and is the cluster most obvious to the naked eye in the night sky.

Qumran: An archaeological site in the West Bank managed by Israel's Qumran National Park. It is located on a dry marl plateau about 1.5 km from the northwestern shore of the Dead Sea, near the Israeli settlement and kibbutz of Kalya.

Saint Joseph of Arimathea: Saint Joseph of Arimathea was the maternal uncle of Jeshua-9/Jesus. Saint Joseph is a wealthy metal trader. He travels long distances during his trading journeys, including the gathering of tin from the British coast (Cannon, 1992).

Saint John the Baptist (Arcturian, Lyran, Sirian): The cousin of Jeshua-9/Jesus.

Saint Peter (Simon): During Jeshua-9/Jesus' earthly ministry, Peter, the Apostle, might have been the most outspoken of the twelve disciples. He indeed became well-known as one of the boldest evangelists. The Apostle Peter certainly had humble origins. He was born in 1 BC and died around AD 67. Simon was the Apostle Peter's given name. It was Jeshua-9/Jesus who gave Apostle Peter his new name. Peter, the Apostle, was a Galilean fisherman and Andrew's brother. The brothers, Andrew and Peter, were from Bethsaida, according to John 1:43 and John 12:21. Peter, the Apostle, was married and was also a follower of John the Baptist.[103]

Samaria: A historical and Biblical name used for the central region of the ancient Land of Israel.

Serres-Egyptians: Lineage of the Hibiru/Hebrew people and the Melchizedek Cloister Host Matrix.

Seventh Root Race: there are seven Root Races or evolutionary cycles through which Humanity evolves. The seventh root race will arise from the seventh subrace of the sixth root race on the future continent.

Tower of Babel, located in Baghdad–Iraq: The Tower of Babel narrative in Genesis 11:1–9 is an origin myth meant to explain why the world's peoples speak different languages. According to the story, a united Humanity in the generations following the Great Flood, speaking a single language and migrating westward, comes to the land of Shinar.

Twelve Essene Tribes: The Emerald founder records reveal that there are Twelve Essene Tribes that make up the entirety of the collective Human gene pool or are the descendants of Universal tribal shield that has been originally incarnated onto this planet from the future timelines of Terra. Each of the Twelve Tribes are genetically key coded to their demographic

Planetary Gates location and to that planetary dimensional sphere and its ley line network.

When Humans incarnate onto a planet, we have genetic time codes in our DNA related to the planetary gates dimensional system that is a part of our main Human Tribal Identity. We activate our Human tribal identity personal planetary keys when we activate our *Inner Christos* by running the 12D Ray, stringing 144 harmonics throughout our Light Body (Body double), otherwise called the 12D shield (shield of the Arc). That identity has had many lifetimes that have participated with the consciousness evolution cycles of assembling DNA codes in the angelic Human Root Races evolving throughout the Solar System.

Light Body Double

The Light Body double is another vessel that sits beyond the dreamtime self. This vessel is in a completely different nonphysical semi-etheric reality that is fourth dimensional in frequency. This reality is by and large so separated off that ascending Humans rarely connect or commune with themselves upon this plane of reality. It is as the physical ascends enough to merge with the Light Body body-double planes that ascension to the fifth dimension shall occur, as it was as these vessels separated that the fall into the third dimension was made manifest.

The Chakras of one's Light Body double are the global Chakras associated with one's field. The global-sized Chakras are sustained by the Light Body double awareness. Occasionally, a person may become conscious of a shattering of their global Chakras. If this is the case, one can report the problem to a healing temple known as The Temple of Light Body. Through this temple is a sharing of records between the physical and oneself upon the Light Body planes of reality can occur.

The dreamtime self is prohibited from crossing over into the planes associated with the Light Body double. For a long time, there were no boundaries, and Humans in the physical were stripping their Light Body body-double of grid work to create false ascensions. Also, many in the physical who had become diseased with such patterning as MS were losing their grid work to false ascents occurring upon the Light Body body-double planes. This is being prevented at this time (except for Karmic circumstance), and there are global guardians between the two realities.

Ascension parallels between physical and the Light Body double self. If the physical is restricted, then the Light Body double is restricted to a level of evolution that parallels in this lifetime. This has assisted in limiting false ascension upon either plane as the two bodies can only be so many vibrational bandwidths apart in frequency as assessed by the ascension counsels. This restriction acts to prevent massive space between that can then be used to prevent global ascension from inside the Human dream.

The false ascensions have been primarily used to inflate space between so vastly that the false gods could then shatter Earth and nature into a fall in consciousness or extinction. As the space between is minimized even further upon the physical and Light Body planes, the possibility of false ascension also minimizes. This is why this is such a prime focus at this time.

The Covenant of Palaidor

The original Twelve Essene Tribes were seeded on the Earth as a part of the evolution plan that was the result of The Covenant of Palaidor to rescue the lost Souls of Terra, making it easier to reclaim these identities when the stargates finally opened during the end of the Ascension cycle.[104]

Twelfth DNA strand: Twelve-stranded DNA is a complex structure which consists, as the name indicates, of **twelve strands**. This particular change in **DNA** structure is seen as a phenomenal mutation that might lead to equally phenomenal evolution.

Ascension Levels of Development

The Light Body Experiment

The purpose of Human embodiments is to attain the State of the Christ or a Vibrational Steward to support Mother Earth in her Ascension to becoming a Star. Many prophets of the past have written about the upcoming Earth movements and devastations awaiting us at this time within our history. However, these Earth devastations are being held in check by those who are embodying the vibrations of Unconditional Love as they support Earth in her Ascension.

The Process of Attaining the State of the Christ or Embodying the Frequency of Unconditional Love.

The process of attaining the State of *Christ* or embodying the frequency of Unconditional Love is the road map of energetic changes that, when complete, allows an embodiment to resonate at the vibration of Unconditional Love.

Each person's experience of the ascension process will be unique unto themselves, as each person has their own genetic memories, past life soul memories, and personal life dramas that are impacted along the way.

Before we get into the details of this phase of ascension, we would like to address why the Light Body experiment is a necessary one on Earth. Five billion years ago, there was a *Fall*. Many are familiar with the *Fall of Man* or the *Fall of Atlantis*. This *Fall* that we are speaking of is the *Fall of all Creations* further into density or matter than had ever been previously experienced. This *Fall* was the result of an experiment that backfired. The purpose of the experiment was to speed up evolution.

The result was a tear between creations that resulted in the destruction of portions of each of the creations and a separation of each Creator, including Humans, who are the creators and part of All That Is or God/Goddess in form, from our Source, i.e., the experience of separation from God.

Our creation is not the only creation that exists. Our creation is only one of 144 other creations. We are creation number 143, to be exact. Beyond each of the 144 creations exists another Creator God known as the Omnipresent One that embraces all of the 144 creations.

The Light Body experiment on Earth was originated within the Omnipresent One by many who feel Karmically responsible for the backfired experiment that resulted within the fall of all creations.

Many parts of the Omnipresent One (144,000 to be exact) descended into this creation to bring the Light Body experiment on Earth to fruition. Those who developed the Light Body experiment knew that every living thing within any creation records all occurrences that have ever occurred within that creation.

Built into our cellular structure is not only a record of everything that has ever occurred on Earth but everything that has ever occurred within this entire creation. As Humanity's cellular structure is restored and healed, our entire creation can be restored and healed along with Humanity.

The third dimension vibrates at such a slow rate that the distortions, imbalances, and disharmony can be readily seen and corrected within our third dimensional energy systems. The same distortion, imbalance, and disharmony exists in the other dimensions as well, but because they vibrate at a faster rate, the distortions often go undetected.

A good analogy for this is that the third dimension is equivalent to taking a movie and slowing it down to a single picture frame at a time. The design of a single frame can be examined in great detail, and many of the observances that would have been missed as the movie was set in motion are now detectible.

As Humankind embraces the fifth dimension and heals their experience of separation from God, the Creator of our Creation heals his/her separation from his/her God or the Omnipresent One. Furthermore, as the distortions that caused a fall into density or matter are healed within the Human form, parallel distortions within our creation, parallel creations, and within the Omnipresent One that resulted in the *Fall of Creation* are healed simultaneously.

This is why the Light Body Experiment on Earth is considered of such great importance and is so closely watched by beings from other galaxies and dimensions. As we embody the fifth dimension, fifth dimensional beings can heal parallel distortions in their own energetic patterning that will enable them to embody their next evolutionary leap into the twelfth dimension. We truly are all healing together.

Nothing within all of creation is perfect. Nor is any Master or being on any plane of reality beyond some level of distortion. Unfortunately, it is Human nature to see the Masters as perfect. All of the problems on Earth exist throughout creation in some form. In other words, as we on Earth heal and embrace Unconditional Love in all areas of both the individual and collective consciousness, so do all others. In becoming *Christed*, one embodies Unconditional Love.

What Does This Really Mean?

It means that you will view yourself as equal to anything and everything within all of creation, whether it be a Master on the nonphysical plane, a Guru on the physical plane, or someone stuck in third dimensional thoughtform. As you accept and have compassion for your own seeming imperfections, you will have compassion for the imperfections of others.

Was the Experiment That Caused the "Fall of Creation "a Mistake?

Of course not. It was a part of the evolution of All That Is, and in evolving beyond it, we will not need to repeat this experience again.

Ascension Levels of Development Initiations 1–6
(Ascension is capitalized to signify a process).

There has been much written about the process of Ascension and the building of the Light Body. We will review a brief synopsis of the ascension levels of development initiations 1-6.

The process of Ascension is constructed by a series of tests or *Spiritual Initiations* that must be passed, and as each initiation is passed, the initiate embodies a slightly higher vibration. In order to embody a higher vibration, the process of Ascension also involves a gradual cellular detoxifying of fear-based patterning.

Nutritional detoxification programs can also impact Ascension and speed up the process but are not an absolute requirement. In an energetic synopsis from a clairvoyant perspective, there are Chakras that extend from the physical embodiment all the way up the 144 dimensions of this creation and beyond.

Our physical embodiment exists on the third dimension, and if you liken spiritual evolution to a spiral with 144 circular revolutions, the next spiral up contains fifth dimensional life form. There are a total of 380 Chakras between the third and fifth dimensions. As the embodiment increases in vibration, more of the *soul* or these Chakras descend into the body.

In the first phase of Ascension, 48 Chakras descend into the body, causing the auric field to grow in size, enabling the formation of a Light Body. The Light Body enables the physical form to begin to hold a new vibration on Earth. The first six Initiations involve the formation of the Light Body. However, it will require many more initiations to embody all 380 Chakras to take Humanity into the fifth dimension. The following is a brief description of each of the six initiations involved in Ascension:

- **First Initiation:** Mastery over the physical vehicle. This is usually passed in early childhood.
- **Second Initiation:** Mastery over the emotional body. During this process, some control over the emotional extremes that may lead to an overly addictive life experience (such as alcohol or drug abuse) is transcended.
- **Third Initiation:** Mastery over the mental body. Within this initiation, some support of one's soul's purpose on Earth comes under the direction of the mental faculties of the initiate. A portion of the Ego is relinquished as the lower will is surrendered. A portion of the soul descends into the physical embodiment as the vibration is now high enough to hold it.
- **Fourth Initiation:** Renunciation. During this initiation, the foundation of fear that an initiate bases his or her existence on is relinquished, and a new foundation is constructed. Oftentimes, initiates experience a change

of job or the end of a long-term marriage or some other type of partnership during this initiation. In the process, more of the soul descends into the body.

- **Fifth Initiation:** Freedom from Blindness. During this initiation, the initiate receives a new direction and better understanding of past occurrences within their lives. In a sense, it is a rebirth into the new following a death of the old. In the process, more of the soul descends into the body, and when complete, the initiate has a fully formed Light Body, but it is yet to be activated to spin.
- **Sixth Initiation:** Activating the Light Body. From a clairvoyant perspective, the Light Body is two inverted pyramids that create a Star of David or a six-pointed star that surrounds the physical vehicle. In the process of taking this initiation, another segment of soul descends into the body, and the Light Body is kicked into motion. As the Light Body spins, it expands in size and enables the physical vehicle to hold a higher vibration on Earth.

Although the sixth initiation brings about an increase in vibration, the initiate is still six additional initiations away from fully embodying the vibration of Unconditional Love. (Please note that the Star of David is the Mer-ka-ba, which is of electrical energy signature. No being running such signatures to any great amount will pass through the Great Central Sun filters alive. By Initiation 3000, an 80 percent detoxification of electrical thoughtform and energy signatures are required).

In other words, the sixth Initiation itself is a halfway point in embracing the State of the *Christ*. Prior to completion of the sixth initiation, the initiate matches the lower vibration of the rest of Humanity.

Following the sixth level initiation which enables the activation of the Light Body, the initiate now holds a higher vibration. As the initiate moves out into the world, all of those who come into contact with the new vibration now match the higher vibration. This forces those who live or work with the initiate to begin to change. One sixth-level initiate in an office will facilitate change within that entire office. Several sixth-level initiates within a large corporation will facilitate change within the entire corporation.

This is all simply due to the new vibration that has been introduced. As a result, initiates often experience a shift in friendships, marriage, or work following the completion of the sixth initiation. Only those who can resonate with the new vibration will be attracted to the initiate.

Up until a decade ago, it was very difficult for almost anyone in Human form to move beyond the second Spiritual Initiation. This was simply as a result of missing information.

If you liken our current life form to have an operating system based on fear, and the new operating system based on Unconditional Love being a necessity for Ascension, the missing information surrounding the new operating system must be made available. This missing information, when supplied to an initiate's Akashic Records, which is our operating system, quickly results in a rapid movement toward completing the sixth

Spiritual Initiation. We currently have over 10 million people on the face of the Earth who have completed this initiation.

Attaining the State of a Vibrational Steward Beyond the Sixth Initiation

Initiations Seven to Twelve

The next segment of Ascension covers the six additional level initiations leading to the State of the *Christ* or embodying the vibration of Unconditional Love. Those who are undergoing this process at this time are doing so in order to begin to fulfill their soul's purpose on Earth and to move into positions of leadership. In a sense, a new wave of leadership is required that is based on Unconditional Love and collaboration rather than fear, competition, and a hierarchical structure.

Leadership will be needed in all walks of life, all industries, all professions, all governmental organizations, and it will be through this new leadership that a restructuring of Human civilization based on Unconditional Love will be brought to fruition.

Many have written about the visitation of other life-forms to our planet as well as intergalactic communication. This will become a reality only as all of Humanity embraces Unconditional Love. Many wish for mass landings of other beings to restructure our civilization for us. We are here to tell you that such intervention would not be based on Unconditional Love, and therefore, would not be allowed within the policy of Intergalactic Law. The only time such intervention would be allowed would be in the event of a nuclear war. Such an event would impact other galaxies, and therefore intervention would be allowed. Even so, such intervention would only be to prevent the nuclear incident, not to restructure our world.

It is within the Human belief system to relate codependently. It is in the very nature of our genetic structure to be dependent on one another and to harbor the wish to blame others and to not take responsibility for the reality that we have created. Completion of the twelfth initiation and embodying Unconditional Love requires that we take full responsibility for every creation within our lifetime. If you believe that something outside of yourself can solve your current dilemma, you relinquish power to another. It is only in understanding that each of us holds the key to all of our own dilemmas that we take our power back and therefore solve the very problem we harbor.

In a sense, completing the twelfth-level initiation means leaving behind codependent patterns forevermore. As all of Humanity embraces their twelfth spiritual initiation, Human civilization will be based on Unconditional Love.

Although this may not be possible within all of the current generations of embodiments on Earth, this will be a reality for the generations that follow. The restructuring of civilization on Earth will be a gradual process, and each of us are extended an invitation to play our part.

The following is a detailed account of initiations seven through twelve or Ascension to the State of the *Christ*.

In completing this phase of Ascension, additional soul segments equivalent to 120 Chakras are embodied. There are 380 Chakras to be embodied in order to embrace a fifth dimensional lifeform. This is still less than one half of the Chakras necessary to make the transition. In attaining the State of the *Christ* within an embodiment, segments of soul descend that vibrate in the frequencies of each of the seven rays within our third dimensional form.

Without going into great detail, much like a prism or rainbow, our civilization is based upon seven main vibrations or rays that descend from the unified source that embraces all of the rays at once. Unification of all of the seven rays is the vibration of Unconditional Love, which is the eighth Ray and is magenta in color.

As the initiate reaches the point of resonating in Unconditional Love, all seven rays become unified within the embodiment, and the auric field becomes a rich magenta in color. To unify the seven rays in the eighth initiation, ten additional strands of DNA must be connected within the embodiment, making a total of twelve working strands of DNA. The connection of the DNA is completed by running frequencies that emulate the Photon Belt in vibration through the initiate's body at night while asleep. It is through the assistance of the teams of Angels from the Great Central Sun from which the Photon Belt emanates that this becomes possible.

For those who do not know, it is the Photon Belt's energy field that will gradually shift Humanity into the fifth dimension. In a sense, those attaining the State of the *Christ* are partaking in this shift ahead of time in order to assist Mother Earth in her Ascension as well as to lead or pave the way for the rest of Humanity.

Seventh Initiation: Transcending Planetary Law. During this initiation, any remaining earthbound Karma is transmuted. Another segment of soul descends into the body and allows for the creation of a new Chakra system.

In the process of receiving a new Chakra system, the information for the ten additional strands of DNA that lead to embodying a state of Unconditional Love are transferred from the etheric body to the physical vehicle. Although the information is transferred, none of the circuitry for the new DNA has been connected within the body but will be connected within the level initiations eight through twelve.

The new Chakra system not only has a distinct new pattern within the embodiment, but the Chakras themselves have the ability to both send and receive information. The Chakra system prior to the seventh initiation can receive only, which prevents a sense of connecting with another and contributes to the sense of loneliness and isolation prevalent within Humanity. The new Chakra system allows for both sending and receiving, enabling the experience of connection or intimacy.

In the final steps of the seventh initiation, three seals known as the seventh seal (Seals of the Arc of Amenti and Sphere of Palaidor) that cover the crown Chakra are removed, which results in a new sense of unity and oneness with all of life. The last step in the seventh level initiation is a surrender of the initiate to serve the divine plan above all else, resulting in access to the Arc of the Covenant, the Universal Tribal Shield, the

Shield of the Arc (12D shield), and one's own unique planetary keys.

Eighth Initiation: Transcending Solar Law. The eighth initiation is one of the lengthiest initiations within this phase of Ascension. During this process, DNA strands two through eight are connected within the body, and all fear-based programming is relinquished. The ego and negative ego are brought into alignment to serve one's soul's purpose on Earth, and duality and polarity are transcended. Two large segments of soul descend to sit within the embodiment, one halfway through the initiations as the fifth strand of DNA is connected, and another just prior to the end of the initiation.

The ego and negative ego have run the Human drama on Earth for over 40,000 years. The ego is the part of us that creates based on personal will, seeks to control everything and everyone, and believes that it is superior and everyone else inferior. The negative ego, in contrast, is the part of us that seeks to destroy or sabotage, relinquishes control to everything and everyone, and believes that it is inferior to everyone else.

The Human personality, prior to the sixth initiation, is comprised of just the ego and negative ego, and the Human dramas are simply a result of the experience of duality or the swinging between these two contrasting parts of the persona.

Following the sixth initiation, another aspect to the initiate's persona comes forth known as Spirit. Spirit seeks neither to create nor destroy, but to co-create the divine plan with God Goddess All That Is. Spirit never controls but rather allows everyone their own drama and sees itself as equal to all others.

By the end of the eighth-level initiation, the vast majority of the ego and negative ego are dismantled allowing the new aspect of spirit to govern the majority of one's existence.

Duality and polarity cause the swings of experiences within the Human drama from controlling or victimizing through the patterns of the ego, to that of being controlled or victimized through the patterns of the negative ego, back to controlling and victimizing again via the ego. Polarity also keeps in motion the experience of joy, followed by pain, followed by joy again. As polarity is transcended, it allows the initiate to move beyond the swings of the ego and negative ego into the experience of the Spirit, which is a more consistent state of joy or bliss.

It is the pull of the planets within our astrological system that have been based on fear that keeps the swing from ego to negative ego and pain to joy in motion within the current Human drama. The eighth-level initiate transcends their birth chart and the pull of the planets based on fear. This is not to say that the planets do not continue to have an influence over the initiate but that the influence is based on Unconditional Love rather than fear.

In completing the eighth initiation, the two minor Chakras that sit above the head that represent the ego and negative ego are dismantled and moved to sit on either side of the heart Chakra and represent the divine feminine and masculine within.

The new inner masculine seeks to create only in resonance with God Goddess All That Is. The new inner feminine seeks to navigate that which is created such that it is in alignment with the Divine Plan. The final step is a surrender to God Goddess All That Is, and one attains co-creator status on a Solar level.

Ninth Initiation: Transcending Universal Law. During the ninth initiation, the initiate transcends seven Universal belief systems, and the ninth strand of DNA is connected. All Karma of a Universal nature must be released during this initiation. Two large segments of soul are embraced by the embodiment.

The seven Universal belief systems are as follows:

Law 1: The law of separation from God Goddess All That Is. As this law is transcended, a deeper sense of unity with God Goddess All That Is prevails. The initiate also attains co-creator status on a Universal Level.

Law 2: The law of energetic balance. It is the law of energetic balance that keeps the swing of the pendulum within the experience of duality in motion. As energetic balance is transcended, the initiate's life is brought to a deeper level of harmony and balance.

Law 3: The law of Karma or indebtedness. As this law is transcended, our sense of owing another to subsist is relinquished.

Law 4: The law of coming and going. It is Universal policy that souls can come together for only a certain length of time or incarnation, and then must separate to experience other encounters with other souls. As coming and going is transcended, souls who are destined to come together to complete tasks on Earth can do so without restriction.

Law 5: The law of female inferiority.

Law 6: The law of male superiority. The feminine energies and skills have been devalued, and the masculine energies and skills have been overvalued within our Universe as well as on Planet Earth. As Laws 5 and 6 are transcended, it allows for more of a balance between the masculine and feminine within.

Law 7: The law of good and evil, light and dark. As this law is transcended, the tendency to see the world in black and white, good and evil is unified, and a portion of the initiate's dark side is embraced.

Tenth Initiation: The Magician. During the tenth initiation, the tenth strand of DNA is connected, and one attains the state of the Magician.

This enables the initiate to transmute energy with a thought from a lower vibration such as pain to a higher vibration such as Unconditional Love. During the tenth initiation, more large segments of soul descend into the body.

Eleventh Initiation: The Sage or Prophet. During the eleventh initiation, the eleventh strand of DNA is connected, and one attains the state of the Sage or Prophet. This enables the initiate to see and know their own soul path more clearly. During the process, more large segments of soul descend.

Twelfth Initiation: Attaining the State of the *Christ*. During the twelfth initiation, the twelfth strand of DNA is connected, and the initiate embodies the frequency of Unconditional Love. During the process, another large segment of soul descends. When complete, one attains co-creator status on a cosmic level.

Due to the vast amount of soul that has been embodied, the auric field of one who has become *Christed* will cover one half the United States in size.

We will now briefly list the initiation levels 13-16, 17-24, 25-36, 37-48, 40-60, 61-72, 73-90, and 91-108:

Initiations 13-16: Transcending Fear

Initiations 17 - 24: Transcending Personal Archetypes

Initiations 25-36: Transcending Group Archetypes

Initiations 37-48: Transcending Planetary Archetypes - Vibrational Steward

Initiations 49-60: Transcending Solar Archetypes

Initiations 61-72: Transcending Universal Archetypes Enlightenment

Initiations 73-90: Embracing Cosmic Archetypes

Initiations 91-108: Attaining a State of Non-Attachment

Chapter 11

THE WHITE BUFFALO

Stanton (1995) tells us that to the Native Americans the birth of a white buffalo is a symbol of rebirth and world harmony.

As Lakota prophecy is told, one summer, long ago, the seven sacred council fires of the Lakota Oyate nation came together. Every day they sent scouts to look for game, but the scouts found nothing. The people were starving.

Early one morning, the chief sends two of his young hunters to look for game. They search everywhere but can find nothing. Seeing a high hill, they decide to climb the hill in order to look over the whole land. As the two young hunters ascend the hill, they see the figure of what looks like a woman who is floating instead of walking. They realize that the person is *wakan*, holy.

At first the men can make out only a small moving speck and have to squint to see that it is a Human form. But as she comes nearer, they realized that it is a beautiful young woman. She wears a white buckskin outfit, tanned until it shines brightly in the sun. It is embroidered with sacred designs of porcupine quill in radiant colors. This *wakan* stranger is Ptesan-Wi, White Buffalo Woman. In her hands, she carries a large bundle of sage leaves. She wears her hair loose except for a portion on the left side of her face, the rest of her hair is tied up with buffalo fur. Her eyes shine dark and sparkling, with great power in them.

The two young men look at her open-mouthed. One young man desires her and stretches his hand out to touch her. This woman was *Lila wakan* (very sacred) and could not be treated with any disrespect. Lightning instantly strikes the brash young man and burns him up. All that is left of him is a small heap of blackened bones.

White Buffalo Woman.

To the other scout, the White Buffalo Woman says:

Good things I am bringing, something holy to your nation. A message I carry for your people from the Buffalo Nation. Go back to the camp and tell the people to prepare for my arrival. Tell your chief to put up a medicine lodge with twenty-four poles. Let it be made holy for my coming.

This young man returns to the Lakota camp. He tells the chief and the people what the sacred woman requests. So the people put up the big medicine tipi and wait. After four days, the Lakota people see the White Buffalo Woman approaching, carrying her bundle before her. Her wonderful white buckskin dress shines from afar. The chief, Standing Hollow Horn, invites her to enter the medicine lodge. She enters the lodge and circles the interior sunwise. The chief addresses her respectfully, saying: *Sister, we are glad you have come to instruct us.*

White Buffalo Woman tells him what she wants done. In the center of the tipi will be put up an *owanka wakan*, a sacred altar made of red earth, and a buffalo skull with a three-stick rack for a holy item that White Buffalo Woman is to bring. The Lakota chief and his tribe do as she has directed. White Buffalo Woman traces a design with her finger into the smooth red earth of the altar. She teaches the Lakota tribe these sacred steps and then circles the lodge again, sunwise. Halting before the chief, she now opens the bundle. The bundle contains the *Chanumpa*, the sacred pipe. White Buffalo Woman holds the pipe out to the people and allows the tribespeople to study the pipe. She grasps the stem with her right hand and the bowl with her left. This is how the sacred pipe has been held ever since.

Again, the chief speaks, saying: *Sister, we are glad. We have had no meat for some time. All we can give you is water.* They dip some *wacanga* (sweet grass) into a skin bag of water and give it to her. To this day, the Lakota people dip sweet grass or an eagle wing in water and sprinkle it on a person to be purified.

White Buffalo Woman shows the people how to use the pipe. She fills it with *chan-shasha*, red willow-bark tobacco. She walks around the lodge four times after the manner of Anpetu-Wi, the great sun. This represents the circle without end, the sacred hoop, and the road of life. White Buffalo Woman places a dry buffalo chip on the fire and lights the pipe with it. This is *peta-owihankeshni*, the fire without end, and the flame to be passed on from generation to generation. She tells the chief and his tribe that the smoke rising from the bowl is Tunkashila's breath, the living breath of the great Grandfather Mystery.

White Buffalo Woman shows the people the right way to pray, the right words, and the right gestures. She teaches them to sing the pipe-filling song and how to lift the pipe up to the sky, toward Grandfather, and then down toward Grandmother Earth, to Unci, and then to the four directions of the Universe. Together with the people, they are all related, one family. The pipe holds them all together.

With this holy pipe, she says, you will walk like a living prayer. With your feet resting upon the earth and the pipe stem reaching into the sky. Your body forms a living bridge between the Sacred

Beneath and the Sacred Above. Wakan Tanka smiles upon us, because now we are as one: earth, sky, all living things, the two-legged, the four-legged, the winged ones, the trees, and the grasses.

The wooden stem of this *Chanumpa* stands for all that grows on Earth. Twelve feathers hang from the stem (see the Prologue - Twelve Tribes & Gates & Races represented). The backbone joins the bowl and the skull. The Wanblee Galeshka, the spotted eagle, the very sacred bird who is the Great Spirit's messenger and the wisest of all flying ones.

You are joined to all things of the Universe, for they all cry out to Tunkashila. Look at the bowl; engraved in it are seven circles of various sizes. They stand for the seven sacred ceremonies you will practice with this pipe, and for the Oceti Shakowin, the seven sacred campfires of our Lakota nation.

White Buffalo Woman then speaks to the women, telling them that it is the work of their hands and the fruit of their bodies that keeps the people alive. *You are from Mother Earth,* she tells them. *What you are doing is as great as what the warriors do.* White Buffalo Woman teaches the people that death is a sacred day when the Human spirit is released to The Great Spirit.

Therefore, the sacred pipe is also something that binds men and women together in a circle of love. It is the one holy object in the making of which both men and women have a hand.

The men carve the bowl and make the stem; the women decorate it with bands of colored porcupine quills. When a man takes a wife, they both hold the pipe at the same time, and red trade cloth is wound around their hands, thus tying them together for life.

White Buffalo Woman also talks to the children because they have an understanding beyond their years. She tells the children that their parents remember being little once, and that they, the children, will grow up to have little ones of their own.

White Buffalo Woman.

White Buffalo Woman tells the children:

You are the coming generation; that is why you are the most important and precious ones. Some day you will hold this pipe and smoke it. Some day you will pray with it.

White Buffalo Woman speaks once more to all of the people:

The pipe is alive; it is a red being showing you a red life and a red road. Through the Chanumpa you may talk to Wakan Tanka, the Great Mysterious. She speaks one last time to Standing Hollow Horn, the chief, saying, Remember, this pipe is very sacred. Respect it and it will take you to the end of the road. The four ages of creation are in me. I will come to see you in every generation cycle. I shall come back to you.

The people see White Buffalo Woman walking off in the same direction from which she came, outlined against the red ball of the setting sun. As she leaves, she stops and rolls over four times. The first time, she turns into a black buffalo; the second into a brown one; the third into a red one; and finally, the fourth time she rolls over, she turns into a white buffalo. White Buffalo Woman disappears over the horizon. As soon as she has vanished, buffalo in great herds appear, allowing themselves to be killed so that the people might survive. From this day on, the buffalo furnish the people with everything they need: meat for their food, skins for their clothes and tipis, and bones for their many tools.[105]

White Buffalo Woman in Lakota mythology is a sacred woman of supernatural origin who gave the Lakota their *Seven Sacred Rituals*. Later, the story became attributed to the goddess Wohpe, also known as Whope or Wope.

When Roman Catholic missionaries first came among the Lakota, their stories of the Virgin Mary and Jesus Christ became associated with the legend of White Buffalo Woman. The syncretic practice of identifying Mary with PtesanWi and Jesus Christ with the Chanumpa continues among Lakota Christians to this day.[106]

White Buffalo Woman.

Return of the Great White Buffalo

The buffalo species was once a form of fully conscious guardian of Earth that roamed the land, assisting in moving and balancing energy for Mother Earth. Full consciousness means that each form, each embodiment of buffalo, contained an individual and incarnating soul. Much like the dolphins and whales today, which are the only remaining nonverbal and fully conscious form of species upon Earth, buffalo existed in a similar state of being. Much like whales and dolphins today, which are the vibrational stewards of Earth, buffalo also was once a vibrational steward of the land.

It was as Humankind dropped the first nuclear bombs about 120,000 years ago that the buffalo species lost consciousness. Much like Humankind, buffalo's fields became so distorted it was difficult for soul to engage with the form. Soul resorted to holding buffalo as a group rather than as an individuated and fully conscious species. In so doing, buffalo lost the ability to hold and move energy for Earth upon the land.

Full Consciousness

Many have heard of the coming of the *Great White Buffalo*. Indeed, there are 26 white buffalo that have been born upon Earth to date, the most recent born in April 2024. The first birth began in 1992, and they have produced one white calf somewhere upon Earth per year ever since. The white buffalo represents the return of full consciousness for the species. The production of a white calf should not be possible giving the genetics that they hold, for all hair color for the species has been brown or black for a very long time. The white hair of these newborn buffalos is the result of their conscious choice to override the genetics of the form to produce *white hair*, or hair without pigment. Buffalo's soul has collectively chosen to override the genetics to produce 26 white calves. They do this to give Humankind living proof that soul can consciously alter the genetics of the form.

The return of the white buffalo to Earth represents a time of great transition. All species upon Earth are choosing to ascend at this time. In so choosing to ascend, much like altering the hair color in the follicles of the buffalo form, we are also choosing to transmute our forms to the crystalline cellular structure for the purposes of the restoration of full consciousness within our species.

Full consciousness means that one serves Earth as a whole in all that one does. The buffalo of long ago would roam to regions upon Earth in need of assistance in the movement of energy. Such assistance is both in the physical and in the nonphysical, for just as all form at this juncture of history, buffalo also had individual light bodies. Such light bodies could be projected anywhere upon Earth's surface or upon the many dimensions in which Earth is related for the purposes of assisting in the repair and maintenance of the energy fields necessary to support and sustain life.

At this time, buffalo do not have individual light bodies. However, several decades into the future and with much additional genetic alteration to their species, each buffalo shall be individually incarnated into again and contain an individual Light Body for the purposes of supporting Earth in all manners possible. There are many others likewise choosing this in the evolutionary path ahead including deer, elk, bear, bison, giraffe, elephant, and moose, to name a few.

Why would all species choose the restoration to full consciousness? Earth is ascending. The further Earth moves up in frequency, the more support she shall require in the maintenance of her evolving field as she transitions to a fifth dimensional vessel.

The Red People: Long ago, the red nation Humans received visions from the buffalo species that as the white buffalo returned to Earth, that the time of transition would begin. The transition they speak of is the transition from a third dimensional Earth to a fourth dimensional Earth, and then on to a fifth dimensional world. Such transformation shall not be rapid but has begun, and everything upon Earth is beginning its evolutionary journey *home*. A time awaits ahead that shall be filled with joy as all species, including Humankind, enter the dance of unity and oneness, harmony, and Unconditional Love.

The red nation Humans, along with many Indigenous Humans, hold the keys to remembrance of full consciousness within the Human species, keys to a Human form that lived in unity and harmony with Earth. However, regardless of what genetic package a Human currently has, whether they be white, yellow, black, or red, there is a connection to the time of unity. Perhaps such a connection is not in one's recent ancestry, but in one's ancient ancestry from long ago.

Each Human, just like buffalo, can now choose to consciously alter their genetic structure and begin the journey to full consciousness. One shall accomplish this goal only if one chooses it so and continues to choose it each day, each week, each month, and each year until such a goal is fulfilled upon. Such a shift shall only occur through conscious intent. Humankind must choose to restore their biology to full consciousness if they are going to survive the coming centuries upon Earth.

Earth is rising in frequency more rapidly than ever. The further Earth goes up in vibration, the faster she shall transmute herself into yet a higher vibration. Perhaps those in Human form cannot feel these shifts yet, particularly in the density of our cities. Go into the country, go to a lake, or by an ocean, or by a forest stream, and FEEL. Feel the unity that pours out of nature. Feel the joy of the dance that nature is in.

Changes Ahead: Everything shall change. There is no present negative thoughtform and no present technology that is going to make the shift into the next dimension. Only that which is conscious shall survive. That which is conscious is all species upon Earth, including the plant, animal, mineral, dolphin, whale, and those Humans who are awakening. There is nothing in our current third dimensional world that shall remain as Earth's vibration reaches a high enough vibration to dissolve it. This shall include the buildings that we rely upon, the cement of our roads, the plastic that we contain things in, and the craft and technology that we perceive as so very important. None of it shall be a part of Earth's future in the centuries ahead.

Perhaps if Humanity was more aware and more awakened to the impending change, technology and housing would be developed that could transition. Such housing would need to be alive and evolving itself, such as minerals. Humans in other worlds who have ascended, such as the Sirian Race about 120,000 years ago, have developed such housing that ascended with them. However, Humanity is too lost to remember that it is time to ascend and that there are great changes ahead. Perhaps this is also a blessing, as those who ascend shall be required to not rely upon technology to ascend the form for them. This shall mean that Humanity shall need to learn to consciously transmute the form just as buffalo is learning.

Why does the form require transmutation? The current cellular structure does not hold enough chi. One must be able to build and build in chi in order to move from one dimension to the next.

So a new cellular structure must be created that can hold a higher vibration and more chi. However, such a cellular structure is not new. Our own ancestors held such a structure once long ago. So one simply calls into present time the structure of the past and begins to embody it little by little until one holds increasing higher frequencies day to week to month to year. This is how all species are ascending.

There are many Humans seeded for this awakening and to make this journey to full consciousness. Perhaps you are one that now can understand that it is time to awaken and move forth. Earth needs Humankind to participate in her ascension. Without some of the Human form ascending, not all Karmic records shall be understood, not all history shall come to be known for Earth. This shall create a problem and potential disaster rather than Earth's future ascension.

The Human form, just like buffalo, can be altered through conscious intent. You too can enter a new kingdom, one based upon unity, honor, joy, and Unconditional Love along with all species. The time of the return of the Great White Buffalo has come. Let us move forth together and co-create a new tomorrow based upon joy!

New Communities: Those who are ascending shall retreat together and form new communities of ascending Humans. Such communities shall work hand in hand with nature and all kingdoms upon Earth to be in absolute harmony and yet provide all needs for all concerned. Such communities shall be devoid of most of the technology that Humanity currently relies upon and live a simple life that revolves around the cycles of nature. The simple life allows for time for the inner work, for meditation if you wish, which is required upon the spiritual path. These new communities shall support those in Human form who choose to ascend.

Embrace and Forgive: It is a great truth that there has been much pain inflicted upon Earth, upon her species, and upon Humanity by Humanity. Such experiences, when forgiven, are erased in full from the memory bank of Earth and all ascending species. As such incidents are erased in full, they shall cease to recur again in Earth's future.

We invite Humans not to sit in judgment for past or present wrongdoing by Human sources, but to embrace and forgive. Each Human is a part of the Human species, and each Human therefore has inflicted such atrocities upon nature, upon Earth, and upon one another. One's ancestry is the Human ancestry, and as one forgives themselves and forgives their ancestors for their wrongdoing, a new tomorrow can emerge that is different from the past.

Choose to Ascend: It is Human nature to attempt to change perceived problems upon Earth through uprisings, war, demonstrations, by becoming an advocate for this or that. This is not what we ask, for such thoughtform does not serve. Such thoughtform only causes animosity and hatred between Humans of different beliefs, and this is the root of warfare in the Human dance. Instead, we ask that each Human take responsibility for oneself and choose to ascend, choose to evolve, choose to alter their thoughtform and biology. It is in the choice to ascend that the atrocities of the past and the distorted Human dance in the present shall be resolved. One may wonder, how can this be so? It is so because Earth is a conscious being and is evolving; Earth is ascending. Earth is rising above the thoughtform of right and wrong, victim and victimizer, abuser and abused. In so doing, everything upon Earth must rise above such thoughtform or it shall perish. Therefore, such stands and uprisings are useless, and those participating in such endeavors and choosing not to ascend shall die off in due course.

The vibration of Earth is quickening. As Earth quickens, that which does not quicken with her shall become ill. It shall become ill because there shall be more energy running through the form than the form was designed to handle. As more chi runs through the etheric body, it exacerbates the blockages or stuck regions of form, causing disease to manifest more rapidly than before. The higher in vibration Earth goes, the more rapidly those who are not ascending shall become diseased. In time, and in the next 30 years, we anticipate that there shall be no non-ascending Humans remaining upon Earth.

The technology shall die with those that are attached to it. Those who are ascending shall retreat away from such devices along with the cities of your world. Such density hurts the field of those who are ascending. The frequencies of electricity behind the technology Humankind relies upon hurts her form and field, tearing holes into the subtle bodies. The density in the cities causes such a loss of chi that she can ascend no further living in such regions. So it shall be true for all intent upon the choice to ascend, sooner or later each shall retreat into the country. In so doing, the form and field shall be supported, and one may choose a simpler life upon the land that allows for the meditation and inner focus that self-mastery requires.

Time is running out. Today, we stand upon the precipice of great change, and yet perhaps things seem the same as they have ever been. Once long ago, our ancestors stood upon the precipice of great change and were also told about impending global shifts. Some heeded such warnings, and others chose to ignore it, ending their lives in great travesty. What will you choose today? Will you choose to ascend? Or will you choose the dance of death that lies ahead for those who choose not to rise with Earth in frequency?

Each Human must do their part. Just because Humans are in forgetfulness does not exempt them from the responsibility toward Earth that they inherently agreed upon in coming to live upon this land. Each Human has agreements to support Earth in her choice to ascend. Most Humans are choosing to default upon their agreements in their forgetfulness. We ask you to wake up and remember, choose to ascend, and choose to support Earth in her choice to ascend. World Peace is attainable through ascension.

Ascension brings forth completion. Completion creates a new dream, a new consensus for Earth. There are many advocates for peace; however, the peace they search for shall only be found as Humanity chooses to ascend and chooses to release all Karma for warfare. There is no other way, for all others have failed in the past 120,000 years of Human history. We can honestly say that any other means of creating world peace that is everlasting is not possible without ascension, for all other means have indeed been tried and have indeed failed time and time again.

The World Wars that we know of in our recent history are just a replay of countless other wars in times past of similar nature. The Holocaust and deliberate destruction of countless Human forms is just a repeat of other holocausts too numerous to remember. The dropping of the nuclear bombs on Hiroshima is two of sixteen of such expressions caused by Human warfare, and those earlier in our history were far more devastating, creating nuclear winters killing all plant kingdoms around the globe. As all Karma for warfare from Humanity's past is released in full, there shall be no future war of any kind upon Earth.

How does ascension create world peace? It does so by altering the dream for Earth. The dream is a living breathing consensus reality that has boundaries that state *this can occur upon a global level,* and *this cannot occur upon a global level.* Global level occurrences are complex in their manifestation and let us suffice to say that as Earth transcends destructive thoughtform, there shall be no further destruction of Earth, for Earth shall not allow it.

The Gift of Ascension: As Earth does not allow it, the responsibility for destructive thoughtform returns back upon those that hold on to such thoughtform in their choice not to ascend and transcend. As such, personal destruction shall follow instead. Sometimes it can be made manifest in an accident, a suicide, or a murder. Most of the time, it comes in the form of disease. All disease is the result of destructive thoughtform that has become internalized and cellular. Ascension allows for the transcendence of such thoughtform upon a biological level, and those who are ascending simply bypass such an outcome in their choice. Disease is equated to cells that have died, or are dying, or deliberately killed by other cells known as viruses. In ascension, all cells that have died or are dying are resurrected into the crystalline form. All cells that are viral in nature receive a new blueprint that is supportive rather than destructive to the overall health and well-being of the form. This is the gift of ascension, an ageless and disease-free form that can live to see a new era of peace and unity emerge for Humanity and Earth.

However, such transmutation in ascension is not without known difficulties. Sometimes the difficulties come from a weak organ. We have seen many whales and dolphins beach themselves due to liver failure from an attempt to ascend. So ascension is not a cure-all for disease. In many respects, starting with a healthy body is of the utmost import, for it requires a healthy form to detoxify all of the biological changes inherent in ascension. It is for this reason that we anticipate that only the healthiest members of all species will make it and attain full consciousness. This may mean a drastic reduction of our overall population. However, this is not of import to us, only that some live to make it, as they too shall reproduce increasing the representatives of fully conscious stewards in the future.

Attachment and Loss of Consciousness: For Humanity, this is a difficult thing, so attached has one become to the particular body that one inhabits, along with one's friends and family. Such is the nature of the loss of consciousness, for in such a loss, one fails to see the overall picture and sees life upon Earth only from the limited vantage point of one's individual self. It is in the selfishness and the lack of overall vision that Humanity has become so far out of sync with Earth. This changes in ascension, for as one approaches full consciousness, one begins to perceive the overall dance of the Human species along with all species upon Earth. This gives one another vantage point, another means of relating to one another along with all other species therein.

White Buffalo Agreement with the Red Nation Humans: Long ago, Great White Buffalo agreed with the red nation Humans to assist in the evolution of the Human species. These agreements came hand in hand with the loss of the ed nation Humans land. This loss we speak of is not in recent times, although such history has indeed repeated itself. This loss we speak of was over 154,000 years ago as Lemuria was flooded and most of the red nation Humans drowned. At this juncture, buffalo agreed to support the red nation Humans in the restoration of consciousness, and the restoration of hope for a new future for Earth in her global ascension.

Buffalo work with the red nation Humans today and those that are seeking their Red inheritance, whether they be black, white, or yellow. For all races are related to the original seeded race upon Earth that is indeed Red. Buffalo have shared their visions with the Red brothers and sisters to give them hope, for they indeed lost all hope as the white people took away their land and destroyed their herds in the century past. Buffalo shared with them that another time was coming, another time when the principles for which they stood and remembered would flourish. Indeed, the time is coming. We honor the red nation Humans for holding on to the dream, holding on to the vision, holding on to the TRUTH. We invite all of Red heritage from one's ancient past to become this new dream, live this new vision, and stand in the TRUTH.

The TRUTH supports Earth. The TRUTH honors all species. The TRUTH loves unconditionally. The TRUTH blesses all with the love of God Goddess All That Is. The TRUTH stands not in judgment, but honors all in the dance of life. It is time for the TRUTH to reign again upon Earth.

White Buffalo Woman.

Summary

In review, the ascension timeline outlined in this book shows us that the Anu-Melchizedeks and Templar-Anu are allowed back into the Sphere of Amenti about 3,300 years ago with the birth of the Pharaoh Akhenaton/Amenophis IV. The Hibiru/Hebrew morphogenetic field is realigned and enters into the Sphere of Amenti with the birth of Jesheua-12/Tutankhamen (twelfth-level Avatar). At the present time, all races are part of the ascension process of repairing and assembling various DNA configurations (Amenti morphogenetic field).[107] The ascension mission that is brought to Earth by Jesheua -9/Jesus is still in place. At this time, the collective consciousness is raising for the prophesied *144,000 awakened ones* who are holding a higher vibration in order for those who are ascending to transition home to the Tao. The 144,000 is spoken of in the Book of Revelations, Chapter 7. For those of us who are ready for the ascension process, becoming aware of the many layers of fear that hides our light is an essential part of the ascension process. We will peel off each layer of fear (making it conscious) in order to truly know who we are, beings of light. Personal healing and the releasing of emotional blocks is required to clear our emotional bodies from injuries from our many lifetimes on Earth. There is a type of *burning away* of energetic blocks happening in present time. Due to current cosmic activity streaming into our solar system, there is also a burning away within the atmosphere. The increasing flow of solar winds are activating our codons. The codons, DNA nucleotides that correspond with specific amino acids, are responding to cosmic and environmental shifts of Earth's sun, clearing away parts of us that are no longer needed.

In order to clear our emotional bodies from injuries from many lifetimes on Earth, we must work on healing ourselves. If we are resisting anything in our life, it's time to heal it (what we resist persists). Ascension is about accepting everything and everyone, no exceptions. All consciousness is equal. We are all fragments of the same consciousness, an original source of consciousness. While we are not separate from other souls, each of us has our own unique path of evolution and life lessons. Remember, we are all originally from one source. Therefore, there is no right or wrong, only different degrees of understanding. This understanding releases us from the frequency fence that has held us in the lower 3D for so long.

As we ascend as a collective, the third DNA strands will begin to release the 666 mutation through the lifting of the Frequency Fence, see chapter 2 - Into Egypt: Pyramid of Gizeh: The Seal of Amenti (7-D Seal) & chapter 3 - *The Axion Seal aka Templar-Axion Seal*. Through this process, our perceptions and cognition will integrate with our Higher Self. The subconscious will become more transparent, and our ability to identify our subconscious mind and our ego will be enhanced. As a result of this awareness, there is a conscious connection to our multidimensional selves and an understanding that we are much more than this 3D life. This process corresponds to the final *resurrection from death* that has been a part of many of the world religions. We are collectively raising the vibration of the planet in order to return with Earth back to the Great Central Sun Dream. My advice is to continue to work on loving yourself in all of who you are, from your starseed origins to your Human (egoic) self. Love yourself in both the light and dark aspects of who you are. Remember, you are a light being. Remember, we hold the power of ascension within our DNA.

As a collective, we now hold the power of ascension within our DNA; our sacred journey is the embodiment of the teachings of the Law of One that are unity, peace, and love for one another. The Mayans of South America, Aztecs, Hopi people of the American Southwest, the Bushmen of Africa, the Australian Aboriginal people, Christians, Buddhists, Toltec teachings, Islam, numerous prophets (Edgar Cayce), saints, and mystics throughout the world have foretold of the coming new times. We bless you. We love you. Stand tall in your starseed truth and be well.

> *Love is what will bring us back to the original teachings of the Law of One of unity, peace, Unconditional Love, and compassion. It is up to each individual to complete personal ascension in order to return with Earth back to the Toa and the Great Central Sun Dream.*

Seventh Root Race. The rainbow people will gather.

Bibliography

Ascension dictionary (2019).
https://www.ascensiondictionary.com/#google_vignette

Ascension glossary (2019).
https://ascensionglossary.com/index.php/Main_Page

Asur'Ana (2019; 2020). *Ascension Insights.*
https://aligningwithearth.com

Bowling, C. (2011). *A new order of the ages.* iUniverse, Inc.

Cannon, D. (1992). Jesus and the Essenes. Ozark Mountain Publishing.

Cannon, D. (2011). *The custodians beyond abduction.* Ozark Mountain Publishing.

Cline, E. (2014). 1177 BC. *The year civilization collapsed.* Princeton University Press.

Dupont-Sommer (1961). *The Essene writings from Qumran.* Wiley-Blackwell publishing.

Kenyon, T., Sion, J. (2019). *The Arcturian anthology.* ORB Publishing.

Ferrara, A. (2008). *The fifth world.* On Demand Publishing.

Hawas, Z. (2019). Egyptian Archaeologist, Wikipedia. https://en.wikipedia.org/wiki/ZahiHawass

Henry, W. (2019). The Ark's missing piece. https://www.williamhenry.net

History of Egypt podcast. https://www.egyptianhistorypodcast.com/episode-100b-raising-the-children-high/

Holleman, J. (2016). Was the biblical Moses the same person as thePharaoh Akhenaten? https://www.quora.com/

Hurtak, J. (1996). The book of knowledge: The keys to Enoch 6th edition. Shakespeare and Company Books.

Jorjani, J. (2016). The Irish origins of civilization. http://www.irishoriginsofcivilization.com/cult-of-mithras.html

Ladd, L. (2018; 2019). Ascension guidance. https://www.youtube.com/channel/UCXxn1HpP2HYaRjgqf1MXxoA

Laitman, M. (2002). *Attaining the worlds beyond: A guide to spiritual discovery.* Kabbalah Publishers.

Lysne, R. (2019). The center for the soul. http://www.thecenterforthesoul.com

Mark, J. (2017a). Hyksos, Ancient History Encyclopedia. https://www.ancient.eu/Hyksos/

Mark, J. (2017b). Clergy, priests, and priestesses in Ancient Egypt. https://www.ancient.eu/article/1026/clergy-priests--priestesses-in-ancient-egypt/

Nelson, K. (2016). Edgar Cayce's Hall of Records revealed. https://www.youtube.com/watch?v=4R4F2EpZTuU&list=WL&index=5&t=0s

Osman, A. (2002). *Moses and Akhenaten: The secret history of Egypt at the time of the Exodus.* Simon and Schuster.

Osman, A. (2004). *Jesus in the house of the Pharaohs: The Essene revelations on the historical Jesus.* Bear & Company.

Osman, A. (2014). *The lost city of the Exodus: The archaeological evidence behind the journey out of Egypt.* Bear & Company.

Osman, A. (2019). *The Egyptian origins of King David and the Temple of Solomon.* Bear & Company.

Parkes, S. (2019). https://www.simonparkes.org

Ray, S. (2024). *In the beginning* Vol. 2. Helm Publishing.

Richards, M. (2019). Earth and Planetary Science. https://eps.berkeley.edu/people/mark-richards

Reeves, N. (2016). *The discovery of King Tut* [Video]. https://www.youtube.com/watch?v=kQSSgZ5x370

Roberts, J. (2012). *Seth speaks.* Amber Publishing.

Stanton, J. (1995). *White Buffalo Calf Woman.* https://www.crystalinks.com/buffalocalfwoman.html

Van Tassel, G. (1958). *The council of seven lights.* DeVorss & Co.

Wellman, J. (2019). Apostle Peter Biography: Timeline, life, and death. https://www.whatchristianswanttoknow.com/apostle-peter-biography-timeline-life-and-death/

Winter, D. (2019). *Spiritual science of immortality, aura cleansing, bliss, ETs, and humanities purpose with Dan Winter* [Video]. https://www.youtube.com/watch?v=ezTbrLM9ZOY&list=PL8cZ9vqVXZZbDUorzzth-iaHoZPP4Fg1a&index=2&t=0s

Winter, D. (2000). *The Eggxfiles and bliss practice with Dan Winter* [Video]. https://www.youtube.com/watch?v=u1SCoceLHRU

Appendix

Appendix A

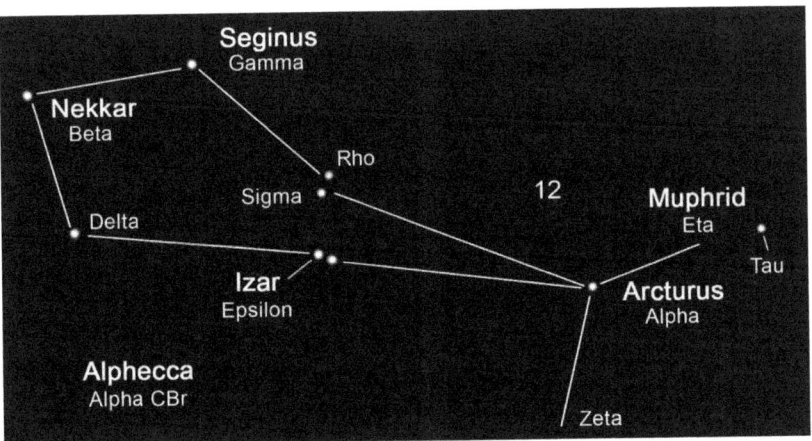

Image showing where Arcturus is located. Arcturus is the fourth brightest star in the sky and the brightest star in the constellation Bootes.

Appendix B

THE BIG STORY OF THE BIBLE
TIMELINE CARDS
© Mark Barry 2008 | visualunit.me
Please do not republish without permission, but feel free to copy for personal use.

 CREATION
GOD SPEAKS THE UNIVERSE INTO EXISTENCE

 ADAM & EVE
GOD CREATES HUMANITY IN HIS IMAGE TO CARE FOR HIS CREATION

 FALL
HUMANITY REJECTS GOD & IS EXPELLED FROM THE GARDEN OF EDEN

 NOAH / FLOOD
GOD FLOODS THE EARTH, YET SAVES & MAKES A COVENANT WITH NOAH & HIS FAMILY

 BABEL
GOD CONFUSES THE LANGUAGE OF THE WORLD & SCATTERS HUMANITY

 ABRAHAM (ISAAC & JACOB)
GOD PROMISES TO BLESS ABRAHAM & ALL PEOPLE THROUGH HIM

 JOSEPH / EGYPT
JOSEPH & HIS BROTHERS MOVE ISRAEL TO EGYPT

 MOSES / EXODUS
THROUGH MOSES, GOD SAVES ISRAEL FROM SLAVERY IN EGYPT

 LAW
GOD MAKES A COVENANT WITH ISRAEL TO BE THEIR GOD

 TABERNACLE
GOD DWELLS WITH ISRAEL IN THE TENT OF MEETING

 WANDERING
ISRAEL WANDERS IN THE DESERT FOR 40 YEARS

 PROMISED LAND
JOSHUA LEADS ISRAEL INTO THE PROMISED LAND OF CANAAN

 JUDGES
GOD RAISES UP JUDGES TO SAVE ISRAEL FROM ITS ENEMIES

 SAUL
SAUL BECOMES ISRAEL'S FIRST KING, BUT DISOBEYS GOD & LOSES HIS KINGSHIP

 DAVID
GOD MAKES A COVENANT WITH DAVID TO ESTABLISH HIS THRONE FOREVER

 SOLOMON/TEMPLE
SOLOMON BUILDS A TEMPLE FOR GOD IN JERUSALEM

Appendix C

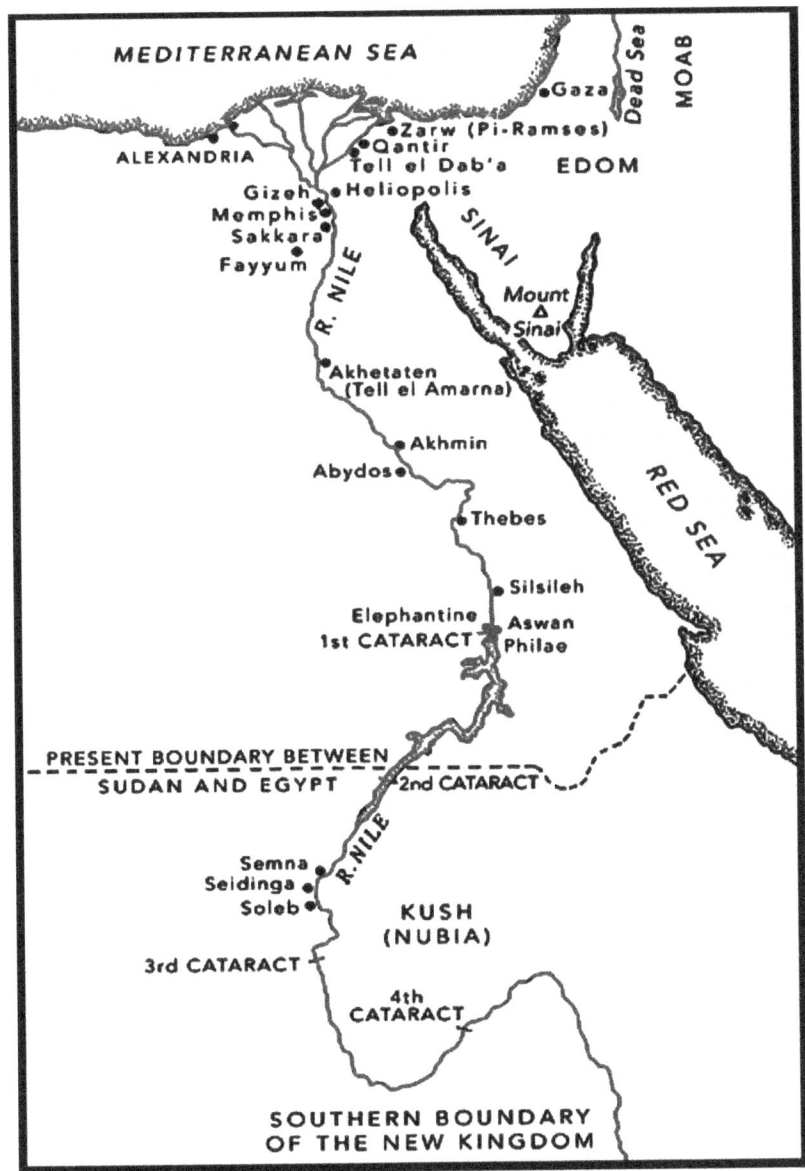

Egypt during the eighteenth dynasty, 15775 to 1335 BC (Osman, 2004).

Appendix D

Limestone Stele of a Priest Roy and his standard-bearer, Kashisha. Egypt, eighteenth dynasty (1420 BC).

Appendix E

Iconography – Egyptian, Mut Muya, Mut.

Appendix F

Egyptian stele, Amun, Ramses I, and Mutnezmet Mut.

Appendix G

THE SEVEN ROOT RACES OF THE TERRESTRIAL COSMIC ERA

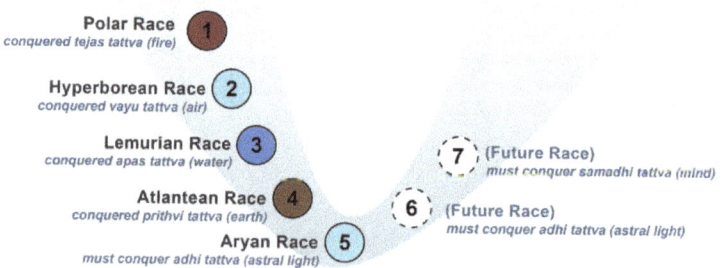

The Seven Root Races According to Hinduism, with Sanskrit Words.

Endnotes

1. LaCroix, 2019
2. LaCroix, 2019
3. Asur'Ana, 2020
4. Asur'Ana, 2020
5. Asur'Ana, 2020
6. Asur'Ana, 2020
7. LaCroix, 2019
8. Richards, 2019
9. Richards, 2019
10. Parkes, 2019
11. Bowling, 2011
12. Hoff, 2019
13. Bowling, 2011
14. LaCroix, 2017
15. Winter, 2019
16. Bowling, 2011
17. Kenyon & Sion, 2019
18. Kenyon & Sion, 2019
19. Van Tassel, 1958

20 Van Tassel, 1958
21 Ferrara, 2008; Nelson, 2015
22 Ladd, 2018; Winter, 2019
23 Asur'Ana, 2020
24 Asur'Ana, 2020
25 LaCroix, 2019
26 Cannon, 1992
27 Bowling, 2011
28 Ascension glossary, 2015
29 LaCroix, 2019
30 Ascension glossary, 2015
31 Ferrara, 2018
32 Ladd, 2018; Parkes, 2019; Winter, 2019
33 Parkes, 2019; Winter, 2019
34 Nelson, 2015; Parkes, 2019; Winter, 2019
35 Nelson, 2015
36 Van Tassel, 1958
37 Winter, 2019
38 Ferrara, 2008
39 Nelson, 2015, p. 608
40 Bowling, 2011
41 Winters, 2019
42 Osman, 2019
43 Osman, 2019
44 Osman, 2019
45 Cline, 2014

46 LaCroix, 2019

47 Osman, 2004

48 Phillips, 2017

49 LaCroix, 2019; Osman, 2004; Hawass, 2019

50 Nobel, 2019

51 Osman, 2004 Hawass, 2019

52 Holleman, 2016; Osman, 2019

53 Osman, 2019

54 Osman, 2019; Hawass, 2019

55 Parkes, 2019; Winter, 2019

56 Parkes, 2019; Winter, 2019

57 Parkes, 2019; Winter, 2019

58 Asur'Ana, 2019

59 Parkes, 2019

60 Asur'Ana, 2019

61 Parkes, 2019

62 Ascension dictionary, 2017

63 Parkes, 2019

64 Parkes, 2019

65 Nobel, 2019

66 Osman, 2004, p.1,168

67 Hawass, 2019; Reeves, 2016

68 Osman, 2004

69 Parkes, 2019

70 Jorjani, 2016

71 Jorjani, 2016

72 Jorjani, 2016
73 Sepher, 2015
74 Osman, 2004, 2019
75 Osman, 2004, p. 237
76 LaCroix, 2019
77 Laitman, 2002; Osman, 2004
78 Cannon, 1992
79 Osman, 2002, 2014
80 Osman, 2004, p. 184
81 Dupont-Sommer, 1961
82 Osman, 2004
83 Osman, 2004
84 Cannon, 2011
85 Nobel, 2019; Parkes, 2019
86 Cannon, 2011, p. 20
87 Mark, 2017a, 2017b
88 Osman, 2004, p. 2749
89 Roberts, 2012
90 Cannon, 2011, p. 157
91 Parkes, 2019
92 Asur'Ana, 2019
93 Ladd, 2019; Parkes, 2019
94 Ladd, 2019; Winter, 2019
95 Parkes, 2019
96 Ladd, 2015, 2019; Parkes, 2019; Winter, 2019
97 Edgar Cayce reading 262-580, Nelson, 2015

98   Ascension glossary, 2019
99   Ascension dictionary, 2019
100 Ascension glossary, 2019
101 Ascension glossary, 2019
102 Ascension glossary, 2019
103 Wellman, 2019
104 Ascension glossary, 2019
105 Stanton, 1995
106 Stanton, 1995
107 Parkes, Ladd, 2019; Winter, 2019

About the Author's Journey

Shakinah is a spiritual intuitive and has been an empath her entire life.

At age twenty-three, Shakinah experienced a profound spiritual emergency, leaving her confused, hospitalized, and medicated. She rejected the Western medical model of mental illness and began a spiritual quest to understand her experience and its purpose. This experience has led her to pursue meditation, ancient studies, work with spiritual teachers, Holotropic Breathwork, and medicine journeys that have provided a deeper understanding of her soul's purpose. Shakinah has continued to experience profound spiritual emergence experiences every ten years like clockwork.

www.ingramcontent.com/pod-product-compliance
Lightning Source LLC
Chambersburg PA
CBHW051037160426
43193CB00010B/974